AN INSTRUMENT OF

GOD'S GRACE

The Story of
Sharing Programs/
Brotherly Aid

by

Glen A. Roth and Glenn M. Lehman

AN INSTRUMENT OF GOD'S GRACE
The Story of Sharing Programs/Brotherly Aid

Printed in the United States of America.

Library of Congress Catalog Card Number: 95-82007

International Standard Book Number: 1-883294-33-9

Printed by
Masthof Press
Route 1, Box 20
Morgantown, PA 19543

Table of Contents

Dedication

In the midst of a changing world, Sharing Programs is one place where a vision, embodied in people and organized 45 years ago, continues to live and thrive. The original vision—*brothers and sisters in Christ helping each other in time of need*—is at the heart of the activities of Sharing Programs. John B. Shenk, an ordained minister, husband, and father of three, played a key role in keeping the vision alive. Throughout his 36 years of service to Sharing Programs, John balanced the demands of family, church, and office. An idealist and a man full of compassion, he has guided Sharing Programs through legal, societal, and church community changes and has seen the organization grow from several hundred to more than 18,000 members. This book, which in part chronicles his years with Sharing Programs, is dedicated to John in acknowledgment of service to his brothers and sisters in Christ.

Preface

The enormous task of writing this history could not have been done alone by Glenn Lehman and Glen Roth whose names appear as authors. They wish to express appreciation for the generous cooperation of the board and staff of Sharing Programs, David Rempel Smucker and the Lancaster Mennonite Historical Society (Lancaster, Pennsylvania), the Archives of the Mennonite Church (Goshen, Indiana), Donald Garber for his copy editing, and many other readers of the manuscript, especially John B. Shenk who checked for historical veracity.

Glen Roth, the administrator of the entire project, took primary responsibility for oral history research, administration of the photographs, proof reading, publishing agenda, illustrations, and index. Glenn Lehman's role was primarily research of printed sources and writing the manuscript.

Background on the Authors

Glen A. Roth is a native of Albany, Oregon. He has had a variety of careers within the Mennonite Church: teacher and principal at Western Mennonite High School, teacher in Somalia, staff person with the Mennonite Board of Education, administrator and personnel counselor at Eastern Mennonite Missions, and pastor at East Chestnut Street Mennonite Church.

Glen has written for various church publications and has co-authored a book, *Shared Burdens—Stories of Caring Practices Among Mennonites* (1993). He is currently employed as director of education and church relations at Sharing Programs.

Glen received his undergraduate degree from Eastern Mennonite University and his masters degree from Pennsylvania State University. He has a PhD from Union Graduate School. Glen and his wife, Annabelle, reside in Lancaster, Pennsylvania and are members of the East Chestnut Street Mennonite Church. They have three married daughters and a son who is a student at Goshen College.

Glenn M. Lehman has held several positions in the church, including editor of the *Lancaster Conference News* for 12 years and development director for the Lancaster Mennonite Historical Society for five years. He has written articles on history for the *Gospel Herald* and has written two previous books, *Johnny Godshall*, a novel (1992), and *You Can Lead Singing* (1995). He currently is employed as executive director of Harmonies Workshop, a church music organization.

Glenn graduated from Lancaster Mennonite High School, Eastern Mennonite University, Chicago Theological Seminary, and Westminster Choir College. With his wife, Dorcas, and two children, Glenn lives in Leola, Pennsylvania and is a member of the East Chestnut Street Mennonite Church.

Foreword

I trace my personal tie to the beginnings of Sharing Programs (earlier known as Brotherly Aid) in the Lancaster Mennonite Conference through relationships with three key players in the story's development: James Hess, my father; Aaron Hess, my grandfather; and Maris Hess, my uncle (by marriage). I think of James, Aaron, and Maris as grassroots Mennonites from backgrounds relatively unknown in the Mennonite world. Marticville, their closest town, wasn't likely to appear in anyone's mental list of significant centers of Mennonite happenings in the 1940s and '50s.

These grassroots men, and others for whom they spoke, found a voice for their concerns within the church. Because the church listened and responded, we now mark 45 years of operation for the Brotherly Aid Plans.

As Glen Roth and I sat with my father at the Mennonite Home in Lancaster recently and talked with him about his part in the beginnings of Sharing Programs, he marveled, "Who would have dreamed that a kitchen table would be the starting place for what has developed?" As my father reflected further, several themes emerged as central in those beginnings.

Lancaster area Mennonites in the 1940s desired an organized plan within the Christian community for bearing one another's burdens. They wanted a plan that harmonized their spiritual values of simplicity and nonconformity, "something that would bind us together in time of need." They felt uncomfortable with commercial insurance plans that might lead to dependence on courts of law for working out loss sharing settlements.

Lancaster area Mennonites desired local ownership of any plans that would be developed. While they knew of plans in other Mennonite communities, these plans seemed too distant to find wide acceptance in the Lancaster community.

Nevertheless, the stories from other parts of the church inspired Lancaster area Mennonites. They read *Gospel Herald*. They talked with Mennonites from Franconia and Hagerstown and with Amish from Morgantown. If other communities were able to develop sharing plans, why couldn't Lancaster?

My father felt especially encouraged by the involvement of more than 800 children and youth several years ago in writing stories and designing posters to illustrate Christian mutual aid. It seemed a sign of hope that the vision for mutual aid would not disappear with his generation.

May the story recorded in this account help keep alive the vision of Christian mutual aid. Perhaps it will even encourage readers to find new ways of implementing this vision in our time.

When Glen Roth and I commented to my father that he must feel a great sense of satisfaction in helping to begin Sharing Programs, he responded, "To God be the glory!" May it be so.

Ernest M. Hess, 1995

1993 East District Mennonite Church fire

Introduction

Fall was in the air. Fire-orange leaves clung to boughs. Some leaves had already fallen in dazzling displays of color, only then to be lost to sight.

It was November 2, 1993. The East District Mennonite Church, a congregation located close to Watsontown, Pennsylvania, went about its life pretty much as usual. A group of women gathered in the church to knot comforters destined for overseas relief. At about 3:30 p.m. they closed the doors behind them.

That evening the ministry team—Sam Corderman, Glen Souder, and Ken Metzler—met to discuss goals and to pray for love and unity in the mission of the congregation. The congregation, founded in 1959, worshipped in a 100-year-old schoolhouse and a recent addition. In 1984 they had built a new wing.

Yet after those comforters of outreach and those prayers of love, some powers of evil broke loose. An arsonist targeted and struck the building. By one o'clock the next morning someone had issued a death sentence to the entire structure. A night-shift employee across the road first saw the flames. Despite the efforts of the local firefighters, little could be saved. One match took $400,000 down with it to ashes.

Later the next morning LaMar Stauffer, the secretary-treasurer of the Brotherly Aid Fire and Storm Plan, received the call. Instantly a network of people, who in faith had agreed to share burdens of fire and storm loss, came to the aid of East District. By November 11, the congregation had in hand a $100,000 check. Cleanup began.[1] Foundations were laid. On December 22, the congregation received their second check—this one for $269,000. The Plan, dreamed of in 1948 and instituted in 1950, had saved untold anguish.

Before East District had been founded, Mennonites clustered in the Lancaster County and related areas of Pennsylvania took stock of their ability to be faithful to each other in the case of material loss. An individual brought a concern to others in the congregation; the congregation brought it to the district; the district asked the blessing of the conference.

The result in April 1950 was a plan to systematically share material losses by fire and storm. Five years later a plan was begun for sharing automobile liability losses. Ten years later, when hospitalization costs began to require more than a personal savings account, the parent board of both Plans investigated that concern and set up an office to handle a denominational plan at the local level.

Now, nearly 50 years after that first layman expressed his concern for his meetinghouse, nearly $1 billion worth of buildings are enrolled in the Fire and Storm Plan, and the Liability Plan has over 30,000 vehicles belonging to 16,300 members.

Newly constructed East District Mennonite Church, 1995

Although the administrative offices of the Plans are located east of Lancaster along the Lincoln Highway, most of the persons who share through these Plans still make their agreements with the Plans in the homes of representatives who are also fellow church members.

This history of Sharing Programs, the corporate umbrella for both the Brotherly Aid Fire and Storm Plan and the Brotherly Aid Liability Plan (for vehicles), attempts to record the origin and growth of these Plans of mutual aid. Fortunately, the initial research begun by Glen A. Roth included taped interviews with a number of individuals involved in the very beginning of the Plans. As of this writing, one of these persons is no longer living, and two can no longer recall details about the beginning and early growth of the Plans.

J. Winfield Fretz,
author of Christian Mutual Aid

These Plans came into being when the church was establishing many other institutions and the economy of the United States was beginning a huge expansion. They were established shortly after Harold S. Bender published *The Anabaptist Vision,* 1943, shortly after J. Winfield Fretz published *Christian Mutual Aid,* 1947. This was the beginning of an era when Mennonite churches adapted in many visible ways to mainstream American culture. That the church gave new institutional form to the economic mutuality of its members confirms the importance Mennonites and related Anabaptist groups have placed on helping one another. It made a concrete statement that theology of community was still important.

We will see that:

• These plans were voluntary and allowed for freedom of conscience for those who did not participate.

• While life insurance was strictly forbidden when the plans began, there was diversity in belief about other forms of insurance.

- Relations with the government were cordial and law-abiding. When the law required proof of financial responsibility, the Liability Plan found a way to provide for its members without compromising its central conviction.

- Plan administrators cooperated with the national Mennonite offices.

- Plan administrators cooperated with other church groups. Today some 25 church groups have members in these plans.

- The plans never sought independence from the church. The first sponsoring committee was appointed by the Bishop Board of the Lancaster Mennonite Conference. Today the Lancaster Mennonite Conference assembly elects the majority of the board members.

The Fire and Storm Plan and the Liability Plan for autos both came into being in the middle of the 20th century. They began within five years after the denomination, the Mennonite Church, authorized the Mennonite Mutual Aid health program.

This account explores forces at work in the church and the world that might suggest why sharing plans in different parts of the larger church came into being almost simultaneously. This story of the birth in Lancaster Mennonite Conference of plans for sharing losses and burdens tries to find meaning in the founding and early years of operation. By accumulating detail and looking for the personal drama, we try to show that one of the earliest Pentecostal actions of the Holy Spirit (Acts 2:44-45) takes place century after century in very ordinary circumstances in response to common-place needs and personalities.

As the story recounts the more recent years, it picks up tempo. The task of adding detail and interpretation to the recent years will be left for future writers.

RULES

—AND—

REGULATIONS

—OF THE—

MENNONITE

MUTUAL AID

ASSOCIATION,

—OF—

LANCASTER COUNTY, PA.

EPHRATA, PA.
YEAGER BROS. PRINTERS.
1886.

Title page for the Mennonite Mutual Aid Association
Ephrata, Pennsylvania, 1886

— Chapter 1 —

Before Brotherly Aid

Some of the Christian churches in Lancaster County, Pennsylvania count the Anabaptists among their spiritual ancestors. Many of them claim the denominational name, Mennonite. These Mennonite churches are the first actors to come on the stage in this story of a Christian mutual aid group that began almost a half century ago.

Anabaptists didn't wait until the 20th century to practice organized ways of sharing property or financial loss. Since 1525, when the Anabaptist movement began, care for one another has been both spontaneous and organized. As early as 1557, candidates for church membership were asked if they were prepared to give of their goods for the benefit of others (Christian or not) in need. Other Christian groups, such as the Hutterites and monastic orders too, emphasized the community aspect of Christ's kingdom.[2]

Until World War II, most members of the Mennonite-related churches in Lancaster County lived by agriculture in a farm and small-town economy. The farming and small-town lifestyle made it possible to help a neighbor fallen on hard times. Tasks such as the wheat or corn harvest required so many hands that neighbors worked in teams from farm to farm. While barn raisings became the favorite subject for photographs to represent the sharing of work and losses, many less visible behaviors in kitchens, around quilt frames, in sick rooms, at births, and during spiritual crises figured just as significantly in keeping and extending the kingdom of God.

Some recurring situations, such as illness and fire loss, required the collection of money (and not just a day's labor) to meet the needs of those who suffered. By the late 19th century several companies of Amish and Mennonites organized to help pay for fire losses and expenses from illness. The Amish Fire Company of the Morgantown area began about 1875 and still survives. Some Mennonites looked outside the church community for support and took policies with insurance companies such as State Farm or Old Guard.

1890s Generation Organizes Aid

In 1893, one year before the Hamilton Watch Company was founded in Lancaster, several Mennonite men of means formed the Mennonite Mutual Fire Insurance Company.[3] "Mennonite" was in its name, but there was no official connection to the church, which in 1900 was only a loose network of people, not an organization. Oral tradition has it that, after the discovery of some questionable financial actions by officers of the company, the leaders of Lancaster Mennonite Conference (headed by Moderator Jacob N. Brubacher) severed any perceived connection to the church rather than tighten the relationship and enlarge the vision. Later, Lloyd Hershey, son of a Lancaster Conference statistician, Henry Hershey, located the company office at the present site in Intercourse. The company changed its name to Mennonite Mutual Insurance Association and reestablished relationships with the church through Mennonite Indemnity, Inc., and the Association of Mennonite Aid Societies.

The day of Lancaster Mennonite Conference as an entity with a mandate to carry out social service, evangelism, and Christian nurture programs was on the horizon but had not yet come.

By 1945, two world wars in two succeeding generations rapidly propelled the U.S. economy, including the farms, toward centralization and industrialization. During World War II conscription forced a choice for normally nonresistant Mennonite young men. As conscientious objectors, most young Mennonite men without farm exemptions chose to go into Civilian Public Service projects, often far away from their home communities, rather than serve in the military. When they returned home, the Mennonite community somehow looked, sounded, and smelled different. Gone, especially after World War I, was a lot of the Pennsylvania German dialect, country air, and occasional cigar aroma. Arrived were the English language (even in preaching), the ringing of telephones, the fumes of gasoline engines, and Armstrong Cork Company odors.

World War I Generation

In the early years of the 20th century, three teenagers came of age who would have a hand in establishing many 20th-century institutions, including plans for mutual assistance—Orie Miller, Elmer Martin, and Stoner Krady.

During World War I, the Ephrata congregation ordained a minister. Seven young men were nominated. One was excused because his membership was in another congregation. Third in age at 26 was a newly-married outsider, Orie Otis Miller, a preacher's son, a native of Indiana, and a graduate of Goshen College. Next in age was Amos Horst at age 25.

Although Orie Miller knew the scientific chances to be exactly one in six, as he looked to his right and left at the profiles of the young grammar school Ephrata boys, he thought it was not a matter of chance but divine guidance that would lead him to the book with the slip of paper. He had studied Bible at Goshen under John Horsch, had been licensed to preach at a mission station during his junior and senior years, and he felt a call to the ministry.

Orie O. and Elta Wolf Miller

In the full meetinghouse and the heavy air on July 20, 1918, everyone's attention focused on the six books that the deacons had scrambled. When it came to Orie's turn to choose, for reasons known only to him he reached past the third book and chose the fourth one. Amos took the one passed over by Orie. The officiating bishop began to check the books to see which contained the lot. Checking carefully one by one, he found it in the book Amos had chosen. Amos was then ordained. Both Amos and Orie walked out of the Ephrata Church with sober hearts. But they didn't walk away from each other. As a layman, Orie would find his work in institutions of the church.[4]

On that ordination day Stoner Krady was finishing his first year of farming close to Elizabethtown. Married one year earlier, Stoner and Frances Krady were expecting a child to be born in November—who later died at three months of age during the influenza epidemic.[5] Elmer Martin was nearly 24 years old. The three would not meet yet.

Orie Miller Attempts a Plan

A number of years passed. By the 1930s, Orie was the executive secretary of Lancaster Conference's mission organization, Eastern Mennonite Board of Missions and Charities. From his desk at Eastern Mennonite Board in the late 1930s, Orie saw a mushrooming of property accumulation by the mission board: from a school in Ybor City, Florida to missionary houses and schools and churches and hospitals in Africa. Why not, he could have reasoned, do insurance in-house? And so he asked Amos Horst to get him a spot on the agenda the day the bishops met at the Rohrerstown meetinghouse

Description of bearer

Height____5____feet____11____inches

Hair____BLACK____

Eyes____BROWN____

Distinguishing marks or features:

X X X

X X X

X X X

Place of birth____MOUNT JOY TOWN-

SHIP, PA.

Date of birth____AUG. 4, 1891

Occupation____FARMER AND

CLERGYMAN

X X X

Henry Erb Lutz

Signature of bearer

This passport is not valid unless signed by the person to whom it has been issued.

Signature of Henry Lutz taken from his passport

in March 1939. He proposed that the conference have a plan to insure loss of mission property.

His agenda item had its fair hearing, but Henry Lutz, the Bishop Board secretary, wrote the sentiment of the group: "We favor that mission properties be not insured, but that an arrangement be made through an emergency fund, which shall cover losses which may occur, not only of mission buildings, but also of our church buildings." In other words, we'll stay informal and spontaneous when disaster strikes. Bishops Noah Risser, Abram Martin, and Henry Lutz were appointed to work with the Eastern Mennonite Board of Missions executive committee to provide such an emergency fund arrangement. Not Amos, though. Amos could help Orie more as a voice with no vested interest.

Grateful to Amos for voting along with the board and giving him the green light, Orie, with the committee, quickly offered a proposal. Rather than a loosely organized emergency fund arrangement, Orie presented the constitution for a complex new organization called "Church Property Aid Plan of the Lancaster Conference." He would borrow phrases from that when he helped found Mennonite Mutual Aid in 1945.

Orie must have thought he had concocted the perfect plan. The Bishop Board would appoint the chair. The mission board, which had the most money at risk, would appoint the treasurer. Weren't all power bases included with a say?

But there was a fatal flaw: the institutional blood ran too thick. The connection to the people was too thin. Also, the bishops saw too much work. Orie, who could live comfortably by a job in his father-in-law's shoe firm while really spending his time in "volunteer" church work, wanted the farmer bishops to make "final determination of claims." The bishops were already meeting some three days before each spring and fall conference. They approved every missionary appointment and reappointment. Counting their monthly meetings and all the communions, funerals, weddings, baptisms, and ordinations, they had half-time volunteer jobs already. They were not ready to take on additional responsibilities of being the "final determination of claims."

Where were the deacons in this? Where was the impulse of the laity? Orie's plan smelled like a typewriter and a mimeograph machine in an office rather than like a farmer and a carpenter talking about helping out a mission station that burned. The polished, typed proposal looked too good to be true.

Amos probably put in some good words for it. But he knew when something was dead in the water.

Henry Lutz, the businessman bishop who was secretary of the Bishop Board, had become a little intrigued by the idea. It seemed like an idea whose time had come. However, after the bishops voted, he wrote for the minutes to show: "Motion was lost."[6]

James H. Hess Ponders Implications

A young minister in his fifth year of pastoral service south of Lancaster heard this action of the Bishop Board reported at the next session

*James H. and Anna Hess
on their wedding day,
October 3, 1934*

of conference. He hardly noticed that rejected proposal amid the rush of other conference voices that day. But James H. Hess (born 1911) subconsciously made a note to himself: If the church had a property plan, why limit it to institutional property? Why not include church members' homes and farms as well?

On May 12, 1941, the Bishop Board authorized James' bishop, Stoner Krady, together with the ministry of the New Danville district (that included James), to organize trustees and buy the Rawlinsville church property. Church property, James realized, was not just the Welsh Mountain Samaritan Home, Millersville Children's Home, the Oreville Mennonite Home, and sheds and mud and pole structures in distant lands, but now right at home. James wondered, If the Rawlinsville property burned, who would pick up the tab? How much of the loss should he personally bear? What choices were available?

And what about his own barn? When he had bought it in 1937, he insured it through Old Guard. Yet he felt uncomfortable with his participation in an insurance company. Why not just trust God?

Anyway, James was busy enough learning to preach and getting his family of young children off to a good start. He had enough to do as father, husband, and minister, plus serving on the new Lancaster Mennonite School board and the Ephrata Bible School board. There were plenty of others to worry about these practical matters. Weren't there?

— Chapter 2 —

New Danville District
Issues Call for Aid Plan

Maybe others cared, but James did not see anyone doing anything about it. These convictions of sharing burdens tumbled around in James Hess's head. He knew his father cared, too. When his father exchanged haircuts with his cousin, Maris Hess, they discussed this.

Fretz Booklet at Byerland

One day in 1947, a booklet by J. Winfield Fretz arrived in James H. Hess's mailbox from the Mennonite Central Committee office in Akron, Pennsylvania. It was called *Christian Mutual Aid*. The names of Amos Horst and Orie Miller were in it as members of the sponsoring committee. As James read the booklet, he recalled the 1939 Bishop Board action of not adopting the mission property plan. He again wondered about the institutional needs of the church in his own district, the church's high school (on whose board he served), and the vulnerability of his own farm.

He passed the booklet to his father, Aaron Hess. The booklet raised issues relevant to protecting the New Danville meetinghouse, an ongoing discussion for Aaron and Maris Hess. These discussions while cutting hair spilled over into the

Christian

Mutual Aid

A Handbook Of
Brotherhood Economics

By
J. Winfield Fretz

MENNONITE CENTRAL COMMITTEE

Christian Mutual Aid *booklet*
written by J. Winfield Fretz

New Danville Mennonite Church

broader church community, striking a chord and rekindling a conviction that developed into a plan.

There was no particular reason that 1948 was the best time to think about insuring the New Danville meetinghouse.[7] It had been standing since 1907, as noted in the Lancaster newspaper that year, which had an article about its dedication service.[8] The reason was not likely Henry Nauman, the new bishop to assist Stoner Krady. He was starting a small construction business. Fire insurance would likely have been an issue of his trade. Maybe the Hess cousins intuitively sensed protection from fire was on Nauman's mind.

David Thomas (left) and the New Danville fire truck

At least they could guess that Nauman would not lightly dismiss the idea if it were raised. Fires happen in any community. There had been a few fires in the New Danville area recently. And it wasn't long before that Dave Newswanger and David Thomas helped to make a new fire engine for the New Danville Fire Company. They helped to order a Ford chassis and then put on a pump.[9]

In any case, Maris Hess knew the question of fire insurance would arise at the next annual New Danville cluster business meeting—with men (women were welcome, too, but seldom came) of secular and religious concern there.

Maris and Rhoda Hess

Maris, being a farmer minister, knew both minds. And he knew, after countless haircuts, of the philosophical mind beneath Aaron's scalp. During their last haircut, just a Friday or two ago, Maris had said, in essence, if I hold the stake will you pound it in? In other words, if I propose that we have a plan to cover fire and storm loss on the church building, will you second it? The scissors kept snipping. The hair kept flying while Aaron nodded almost imperceptibly.

The average lay person did not have many church meetings to attend in 1948. In fact, neither did the average minister, at least by today's standards. There simply were not many church meetings to attend. Most of the congregations of this area sat among farms, many of them owned and farmed by their members, so that they were in a sense parish churches.

In 1948, the *Mennonite Yearbook* was still noting when and how frequently congregations had services. For Mechanic Grove and a few other congregations, one service every week had been the rule for some time. Martindale, Strasburg, and most other congregations held services only every two weeks.

The institutions noted the void and were creating their own subculture of meetings. Lancaster Mennonite School held chapel daily. The mission board was adding farewell services. The East Chestnut Street congregation held a "Worldwide Mission Conference." A "Young People's Christian Life and Service Conference" was held at Lancaster Mennonite School in July 1948.[10]

A lay person might attend or serve on only a few congregational committees. But two times a year a counsel meeting provided the occasion for congregational, conference, and personal renewal of covenant. "Are you at peace with God and your fellow men and desire to take communion?" In addition, most congregations or districts had an annual business meeting to reckon with the physical needs of the meetinghouse and its cemetery and parking lot and perhaps buggy sheds and budget.

It was at such a meeting that the church would first hear about the need for a plan to share property losses.

New Danville Cluster Business Meeting

Wednesday, February 4, 1948 came. The appointed hour for this year's business meeting approached once again just as it had for many generations.

Stoner and Frances Krady

Bishop Daniel Stoner Krady came to the church and parked close to the back door. He noticed his assistant bishop, Henry Nauman, was already there. Both of them were sacrificing a valuable afternoon. Stoner could be working in the bookstore. There wasn't much to do in his garden—where he raised vegetables that he peddled in the seventh ward of Lancaster City—but he could spend time with the seven children. He could be visiting with the 90 members of Vine Street, where "troubles" had been reported to the Bishop Board. He could have worked on an article for J. Lester Brubaker. The 23-year-old editor had requested one for his new series in *Missionary Messenger*, "Thinking With Our Bishops." Bishop Richard Danner had recently defended the office of bishop in that column as "shepherds who have to guard what has been committed to their care."

Henry, perhaps, could spare the afternoon better because construction in February was slow. Even so, he could have worked on the small indoor job for the butcher David Thomas or worked on his books. He could have visited some folks who had expressed interest in future jobs.

Maris and Aaron entered the meetinghouse and noticed about 40 people already seated on the benches. The World War II rationing of gas and rubber used in tires was over, and travel was picking up.

The economy was on the move. A current issue of *Time* magazine had said that in 1947 the U.S. made 17 million radios and 4,794,000 cars and trucks. The U.S. had turned out "well over fifty percent of the known industrial production of the world." The same 92-page issue of *Time* noted that life insurance companies got a $34 million windfall on a tax loophole.

Krady Moderates Meeting

Stoner called the meeting to order. The routine matters were handled. Then, just as Maris had known, one of the trustees asked, in so many words, "Should we not consider getting fire insurance on the New Danville church building?" People at the meeting heard this as a reasonable thought, even though some of their farms and houses were not insured. Heads nodded.

Aaron looked at the building around him. He couldn't calculate the distress he would bear if this structure burned. Here under these rafters he confessed his faith in Christ and his church. Aaron felt the memory of the people in these walls, the successors of the first stone walls erected in 1755. He thought of the faith convictions of his eight generations of spiritual ancestors on this land and his Anabaptist forebears for the two centuries before that in Switzerland as he unself-consciously rose to speak, "Why don't we just have a plan of our own instead of going to secular insurance?"[11]

If Byerland burned, New Danville people would help, and vice versa. And River Corner. But what about the new Rawlinsville property? Stoner Krady as recently as 1941 had convinced the Bishop Board to approve the purchase of that property as a mission outpost of the district. The mission board funds had bought it. Would that make East Chestnut Street, Vine Street, and New Danville just as equally liable?

If they wanted to insure New Danville today, what options did they have? Ask the world to back up their faith, their trust in God? Mennonites in other areas were helping each other. Articles in the *Gospel Herald* over the past decade discussed Mennonites in Franconia starting a plan in 1936. In Virginia, a plan had been in place since 1911. That simple question-proposal couldn't have seemed more spiritual and natural, rooted in the soil along the Conestoga. For a short moment people paused as though hearing a truth for the first time. It wasn't the first time that it became obvious for Stoner. He was there when Orie Miller made his presentation to the Bishop Board in 1939. He had read countless times before communion in his district the Lancaster Conference Rules and Discipline: "Members shall not have life insurance." But that was life insurance. Feeling the care and natural, brotherly concern of farmer Aaron and the sentiments of the trustees around him, suddenly Stoner saw this in a new way. Intuitively he knew that, while a mission board raising this question looked self-serving, a simple farmer could put it through the conference. Some conference leaders might balk, but it was worth a shot.

"Why not have our own plan?" another voice added.

Aaron Hess

"Why not call for a district meeting to look into this?" someone asked after the profundity of the proposal sank in.

Henry looked to Stoner, who was the elder bishop, for some response. Stoner's smile said everything: he liked the idea. He would plan a meeting. He would clear it and promote it with the Bishop Board. And do it right away. No need to convince people of the evil of the age. Nearly everyone in the warm meetinghouse had read J. Paul Graybill's editorial in the January *Missionary Messenger*: "1948 is a crisis year. The church dare not lose her savor." Besides, better to have a meeting before spring plowing begins.

Aaron and Maris might have arranged another haircut as the annual business meeting closed. Some of those leaving might have discussed the latest news about the Truman administration. They might have mentioned the prices of certain farm commodities, along with consternation at the newfangled implements that Allis Chalmers, Farmall, and John Deere were trying to get farmers to buy. But permeating the farewells and the thoughts of these pious country church people was a feeling of security not felt before.

The people from River Corner, New Danville, and Byerland drove home anticipating another meeting soon—because Stoner Krady "was a good pusher of an idea," a contemporary would say of him. If he said, Let's have a meeting, he meant yesterday or today.

— Chapter 3 —

Special Meeting Called
for February 1948

Krady did act with dispatch. Soon the whole district and Lancaster Conference knew about a special meeting set for Saturday, February 28, 1948.

If there had been any doubt that this meeting should have been called, a page-one *Intelligencer Journal* photo on February 17, 1948, showing a fireman treated at a fire in a Philadelphia furniture store that felled 107 firemen, dispelled it. It seemed as though the blast of that conflagration touched off a "heat wave" in Lancaster County. On February 19, the newspaper reported a temperature of 62 degrees in Ephrata.[12] Something was going on beyond the ordinary. Would the Byerland meeting on this day of February follow this pattern?

Following the annual business meeting of the New Danville cluster (including the Byerland, River Corner, and New Danville congregations—Rawlinsville was a mission for business purposes at that time), the winter, the economy, and life were just waiting for the spring thaw.

Byerland Church before 1953 remodeling

Northwest, along the banks of the Susquehanna River, thaw had already produced an ice jam that flooded Washington Boro on February 22. On the same morning five inches of snow fell, bringing to 33 the total number of inches of snowfall since January 1.

The New Danville cluster of congregations that called this special meeting predate the Revolutionary War. Byerland had a meetinghouse in Pequea Township since 1755.[13] In 1948, membership lists showed there were 270 members at New Danville and 218 at Byerland. River Corner and Rawlinsville had 55 and 50, respectively. Pastoring this cluster of churches were only three ordained ministers, James H. Hess, his uncle Maris Hess, and John H. Miller. Henry Nauman was installed as bishop of the New Danville cluster, but only the year before. Stoner Krady had been ordained in 1937 to serve as bishop to the Lancaster district, which encompassed both the Lancaster city churches and the New Danville cluster.[14]

Krady's Enthusiasm

Stoner liked to get things done. He was a good pusher of an idea. But could he follow through, some wondered. Soon after he started the job as superintendent of the Vine Street mission in 1923, he set up a bookstore in the basement of the building in collaboration with John Weaver.

During his years at Eastern Mennonite School, Stoner had observed the Tract Press that John L. Stauffer, EMS president, had used to print his own writings.[15] Some were staunchly against insurance of any kind. He followed that pattern at Vine Street. Although he was not a writer, he printed. At Eastern Mennonite School Stoner was hired as the farmer and received $80 a month year round, "virtually the same rate as teachers," notes Hubert Pellman sardonically in his history of Eastern Mennonite College. The farmhouse where the Kradys lived was the white frame house known in later years as the Art Building.[16] It stood where the new Eastern Mennonite Seminary building now stands. The Kradys moved there in 1920, the year that the first administration building was constructed.

When the New Danville cluster raised the question about insuring the church meetinghouses on February 4, 1948 and voted to ask the ministry to call a district-sponsored meeting to look at this issue, Stoner probably set the date of February 28 with the interested people as they were leaving the meeting. He knew when the Bishop Board met next.

Was it something to do with his enterprising, evangelizing personality that Stoner sensed by intuition that here was a new field of church work to be plowed? Marcus Clemens of the Franconia Mennonite Conference might have led him to think that. One year earlier, on February 12, 1947, Clemens travelled from Souderton, Pennsylvania to ask the bishops if there was interest in Lancaster Conference for auto insurance sponsored by the church.

Stoner remembered the young Clemens, who had just returned from Civilian Public Service. Stoner had been impressed with his bearing and his plain suit made of bankers striped wool. Nevertheless, Stoner's feeling of discomfort at the idea of Lancaster Conference following Franconia Conference matched that of the other bishops. The bishops elected a conference committee—Sem Eby, Howard Greider, and Shelley Musser—to investigate the idea. However, the makeup of the committee seemed to ensure that there would be no movement toward the idea of auto insurance sponsored by the church.

Why was Stoner eager to act one year later? Was it a way to show his interest in the New Danville cluster? Since Noah L. Landis had ordained him as bishop in 1937, his work with the Lancaster cluster of his district had been closer to his heart. After all, Vine Street had been his home church since 1923. When the Lancaster district expressed interest in mission work in Honduras in the late 1940s, he fostered the local interest and translated it into a conference-sponsored program. In his eyes, program grew out of local interest, and central committees merely managed it. So as not to appear in the eyes of New Danville to favor Lancaster, was he now going to bat for the southern tier of his district?

Stoner was a good bishop to have behind this new cause. He was popular. He also was likely to be sensitive to concerns about church sharing because of his own experiences. He brought no social standing from his family. Neither did his wife, Frances, whom he married in 1917. Making ends meet was a constant challenge. Work at the bookstore did little to offset the expenses of raising seven children.[17] Aware of his limited income, several men in the Byerland area bought him a house in Lyndon, which kept him midway between his churches. In 1939 some men from the same area, who thought a bishop ought to have an automobile befitting his status, traded in his old Plymouth and bought him a new Chevy for about $2,000.

Elmer G. Martin Comes to Meeting

It was almost 1:00 p.m. when Stoner watched the locals park their 1930s war-worn black cars under the Byerland sugar maple and Norway maple trees. That hardly any Lancaster cluster people came troubled him a bit.[18]

He waved and nodded when he saw the black Hudson sedan of Elmer Martin, bishop in the Mellinger district, pull in. In 1948 the Hudson was the car you "step down into," the ads proclaimed. Stoner felt a strange kinship with Elmer, his fellow bishop.

In 1937, after an employee had wrecked Elmer's car and there was no insurance, people at Stumptown Mennonite Church bought their minister a

Hudson car similar to the one owned by Elmer G. Martin

new one.[19] Both men knew the grace of receiving charity from the church. Both were born in 1894, only four months apart—Stoner in Rapho Township and Elmer in East Earl Township. Both started grade school when the 20th century dawned, and both married during the first World War. In 1948, at 54 years of age, they were at the height of their wisdom and power in church affairs.

Their similarities did not end there. Stoner moved into Lancaster City because of his job. Elmer moved to Bridgeport (the edge of Lancaster City) from Spring Grove to work at the business his father, Ezra W. Martin, left to his children. (Before Ezra's business had gotten on its feet, Elmer claimed that his father was so poor that he hated to ask him for a dime. When Ezra was 14 years old, someone had given him a steer and told him to butcher it and sell what he couldn't eat. He did just that, and with the money gained he bought two steers to butcher, and slowly the business built up, the story goes.)[20]

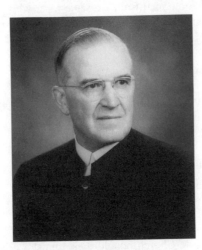

Elmer G. Martin

More people arrived than Stoner expected. He mentally noted four other bishops besides himself. That was one-third of the Bishop Board's 15 (not counting the elderly conference moderator from Juniata County who rarely could attend meetings). Ten ordained men of the

148 ordained ministers and 79 deacons of the conference came. He had hoped for more, but on Saturday afternoon most of the ministers were preparing sermons while they cleaned up the forebay and did other weekend chores on their farms. But all the New Danville cluster's ordained ministry (two bishops, three deacons, and three ministers) were there.

James H. Hess was looking over the crowd, too, and mentally tallied about 50 present, including a handful of guests. He had just seen his brother-in-law, David Thomas, earlier in the week when he was busy getting ready for Saturday market. He would have been glad to see him, but he knew David would not show up.

James came prepared. Coming to meetings with paper and fountain pen in hand was a habit by now. He wouldn't be surprised if Stoner asked him to take minutes, since he was secretary of the New Danville cluster. James was already practiced in the art of taking minutes from his experience as secretary of the Bible school board.

Key Meeting Begins

The meeting began at 1:00 p.m., and for the next few minutes James forgot about writing minutes. Stoner forgot outside distractions. They all lifted their voices and spirits in two-, three-, and occasionally four-part men's chorus singing the Charles Wesley hymn, "Father, I Stretch My Hands to Thee" (*Church Hymnal* no. 371):

> *No other help I know;*
> *If Thou withdraw Thyself from me,*
> *Ah, whither shall I go?*

By verse four the intensity grew: "Author of faith, to Thee I lift my weary, longing eyes."

With this longing for expressing a fuller faith, Stoner rose and called the meeting to order. As James expected, Stoner called on him to serve as secretary. As James took out his fountain pen and put it to the blue-lined paper, a transcendent feeling came over him. He could not have imaged that, 44 years later, he would be standing in an office with almost 30 full-time staff handing that very sheet of paper along with dozens of others to Glen A. Roth, Director of Education and Church Relations at Sharing Programs. (At the time of the 1948 meeting, Glen was in 9th grade at Western Mennonite High School, Salem, Oregon.)[21]

Taking the minutes of that meeting started easily enough. Maris Hess told the group about the earlier meeting where he had proposed a sharing plan. Maris told how the idea for a sharing plan had grown out of the haircut conversations in his cousin Aaron's kitchen and how their wives listened

Father, I Stretch My Hands to Thee

I stretch forth my hands unto Thee.—Ps. 143: 6

CHARLES WESLEY   AZMON C. M.   Arr. from CARL G. GLÄSER

1. Fa - ther, I stretch my hands to Thee, No oth - er help I know;
2. What did Thy on - ly Son en - dure, Be - fore I drew my breath!
3. O Je - sus, could I this be - lieve, I now should feel Thy pow'r;
4. Au - thor of faith, to Thee I lift My wea - ry, long - ing eyes;

If   Thou with-draw Thy - self from me, Ah, whith - er shall I go?
What pain, what la - bor to se - cure My soul from end - less death!
Now my poor soul Thou wouldst re - trieve, Nor let me wait one hour.
O   may I now re - ceive that gift, My soul with - out it dies.

Hymn sung at the special February 28, 1948 meeting that led to the formation of Sharing Programs (called Brotherly Aid in the early years)

and supported them. Maris did not say, but it came to James's mind how J. Winfield Fretz's book, *Christian Mutual Aid*, prompted the conversations.

When Maris finished, the relatively short Stoner called on a tall grocer preacher from the Plains Mennonite Church in Lansdale, Pennsylvania— John E. Lapp of the Franconia Mennonite Conference. Although only 42 years old, John was well-known in Lancaster Conference. He had spoken six years earlier at the dedication of the Lancaster Mennonite School.[22] In fact, he admired the younger but larger sister Lancaster Conference for founding a school and overseas missions program before his conference. Franconia Conference, though, had had a property aid plan since 1936. By 1948, the Franconia plan had 1,000 properties enrolled, with a total valuation of $6 million.

John reminded the Lancaster Conference audience that "mutual aid" (he used that term) is an expression of love, a command, and an opportunity to "share in the ministry of the word." He saw the evangelical and not just the practical aspects of the issues surrounding the concern of the day. Fretz's booklet had not escaped his notice. He also noted that Mennonite writings

-1-

Minutes of a meeting held to consider a
Mutual Aid Insurance Plan.

Byerland Mennonite Church
Saturday Feb. 28, 1948 1:P.M.

The meeting was opened by singing the hymn "Father I Stretch My Hands to Thee". Bro. John D. Risser of Hagerstown, Maryland conduct-ed the devotion by reading IICor. 8 and leading in prayer.

Bro D.S.Krady acted as moderator and he called on James H. Hess to serve as secretary.

Bro. Maris Hess told of the steps that led up to this meeting. He told of a discussion at the recent Business Meeting at River Corner where the question of insuring church buildings was discussed and how one brother proposed a mutual aid plan. He said that the group there voted to hold a later meeting to discuss such a plan and how in preparation for this meeting several groups of brethren from church districts outside our conference, where such a plan is in operation, were invited to be present to give some information.

Representatives from three different groups having such a plan were present. They were from the Franconia Conference, from Washington County Maryland bishop district and from the Conestoga church near Morgantown. Also present were five bishops from the Lancaster conference eight or ten other ordained men and lay members from various parts of the conference within all the New Danville ministry and a number of lay members from this district.

Bro. John E. Lapp of Lansdale, Pa. gave a discussion on the subject, Mutual Aid an Evidence of the New Life. Following are some of the thoughts he presented.
    Mutual Aid is an expression of love.
    Mutual Aid is a command - "bear ye one another's burdens" - "strengthen the weak" - "even Christ pleased not Himself". Mutual Aid presents an opportunity to continually share in the ministry of the Word.
    Ever since its beginning the Mennonite church has been clear on this. Writings of 1557 show that at that time applicants for church membership were asked if they would be willing to give all they had to help their needy brethren.
    Altho the church of that day had no boards nor treasurers they did have deacons who worked conscientiously. They had one fund from which all needs were supplied.
    We need Mutual Aid organizations within the church because of a departure from the faith. We do not do as was done years ago.
    We need Mutual Aid organizations today because people are depending on the State. Worldly organizations are providing all means of insurance and needs.
    It is possible to have a Biblical Church Mutual Aid Organization however we need to be careful. Having a church organization will not develop a conscience against insurance.
    According to Isaiah 58 one purpose of fasting is to have more to give to those who are in need.
    The early apostolic church practiced mutual aid.

Page one of James H. Hess's minutes of the first meeting on February 28, 1948 to consider starting a brotherly aid plan

of 1557 show that applicants for church membership were asked if they would be willing to give all they had to help their needy brethren.

There was no tape recorder at Byerland that day, and James had to write fast to get as much on paper as he could. He was as fascinated with Lapp's ideas as he had been with the Fretz book.

John E. and Edith Lapp and family, 1951

John cautioned the listeners about organizations. People come to depend on the state and worldly organizations. "Having a church organization will not develop a conscience against insurance," he said. He meant that creating a church institution does not guarantee preserving the spirit that the institution was intended to embody.

John, in that age of institutional founding, could have said the same about the Oreville Home, the many missions, Mennonite Central Committee, Civilian Public Service, Eastern Mennonite College. He expounded from Isaiah 58, applying it to the experience of the early church. "Christians should help others without any desire of personal gain," he proclaimed. He paused. That point sank into the mind of James and others; later it would become an organizational motto.

After John finished, his friend, a Brother Kolb, who was also invited to this meeting, explained several details of the Franconia plan. Then Lesher Horst of Hagerstown, Maryland explained the plan he helped direct. The Mennonites in Washington County, Maryland and Franklin County, Pennsylvania had founded their plan some years earlier. They did not provide storm protection, nor did they enroll persons who were in regular insurance companies.

Brother Stoltzfus, an elderly man from Morgantown, spoke of the Amish Aid and Fire Insurance Company, which was started about 1875.[23]

Original Discussion

The afternoon was not young anymore when Stoner opened the meeting for discussion. Landis M. Shertzer, ordained minister at the large 375-member Millersville congregation, had been paying attention, especially to Lesher Horst, and expressed himself in favor of a plan tailored after the Maryland one. He thought it should be based in the conference.

The Hagerstown men were pleased, and John D. Risser stood again and waxed a bit eloquent: "It provides a systematic way to exercise charity. I insure to help you, not for what I get out of it," he said. Several Lancaster Conference people remembered his comments and used "systematic way to exercise charity" later to promote the plan.

James Hess described an Indiana-Michigan plan. Henry Nauman, who was starting a business and knew some of the finer points of insurance, said that he liked the Maryland plan best, but he also liked the reinsuring features of the Franconia plan. He also believed the plan should be based in the conference. There was some concern that if the people attempting to start a plan at a conference level became frustrated they might organize independently.

John Lapp stood again, this time at his bench near the front, and encouraged "going the conference way" and presenting something to conference for action. John Risser affirmed that. The New Danville cluster people unanimously agreed to let what they had started go beyond themselves to the hands of the conference.

Elmer Martin had not spoken yet. Being a practical businessman (he was manager of a meat company, while his brother, Weaver, was president) and sensing the afternoon by now was well spent, he proposed that "this day's work should be recorded and taken to conference for consideration."

The secretary was glad he had a typewriter at home, which his wife could use if his minutes were to be given to the Bishop Board or conference.

Landis Shertzer, sensing that time was short and people soon had to drive home, asked Stoner to "get the voice of the meeting on carrying out Brother Elmer Martin's suggestion."

But Paul Hess suddenly felt things were moving too fast. This was all new to the people from outside the cluster. "Couldn't we go back to our own districts, get feedback and bring that to a future meeting where a plan could be presented to bring to conference?" he asked.

Daniel Wert of the Gingrich Mennonite Church near Lebanon, Pennsylvania was thinking of stopping in to see his cousin Earl if this meeting adjourned in time; he seconded Shertzer's motion.

"Stand if you favor going with Elmer Martin's plan to take our work to conference," Stoner proposed.

Nearly everyone stood. That passed.

Who presents this to the Bishop Board? Someone moved that the Chair Stoner and Secretary James H. Hess do it.

Stoner hemmed and hawed a little bit. Not a risk-taker, he promoted an idea when others put their weight behind it. Besides, people didn't really see him as an advocate for "insurance." In fact, he often spoke against it. He was here because it was his district and it was his duty. He was pretty sure James would do all the work, but two people didn't sound right for a committee. What about Nauman? But his health was in doubt, even as young as he was. He looked over Elmer's way as though asking for help and called for the question. That motion lost.

Deacon Gideon Fisher of the Lancaster cluster wanted to make this look like more than a one-district concern; he knew that Stoner was not perceived as a businessman. He suggested that Elmer Martin go with them, knowing Elmer had the confidence of the bishops and had oversight of the largest congregation, Mellinger.

Landis Shertzer seconded this and it passed. The core group—Stoner Krady, James H. Hess, and Elmer Martin—would see this through.

Brother Elvin Herr, another deacon in the New Danville cluster, expressed hope that the Bishop Board would respond one way or the other.

The group was beginning to stir.

Stoner expressed appreciation for those who came from a distance for their help and called on Bishop Simon Bucher from the Lebanon district to give the benediction. Stoner was glad Simon was there.

A door had opened for something to begin. Would it?

— Chapter 4 —

Plan Takes Shape at Vine Street

Founding Team Established

Begin it did! October 13, 1948 to March 28, 1950 was the year of the "Committee to Plan Brotherly Aid,"* as the minutes stated. The committee members included the three appointed by the meeting at Byerland and affirmed by the Bishop Board: Bishop Stoner Krady, Bishop Elmer G. Martin, and Minister James H. Hess. In addition, there were four others chosen by the Bishop Board: deacons Galen Hostetter, Isaac King, Andrew Shaub, and a layman—David Z. Weaver. Simon Bucher would be added five months later. The committee would take a proposal to two public meetings, send it to all ordained leaders, and sit on it 13 evenings at Vine Street. But would the egg hatch?[24]

Isaac and Rebecca King

In Andrew H. Shaub the committee found a deacon from the Rohrerstown congregation, the son of a trustee. Isaac S. King, also a deacon, ministered at Millwood, which had just been annexed onto the Lancaster Conference fold. (In 1948 five of the six ministers in the Millwood district were named Stoltzfus. The sixth was a young, conscientious minister, Noah L. Hershey, Jr., at the Parkesburg congregation. One day he would moderate the conference when it gave approval to moving the conference office to its present location.)

*The committee that did the initial work of organizing the Brotherly Aid Plans was known variously as the Committee to Plan Brotherly Aid, the Standing Committee, the Executive Committee, the Advisory Committee, and the Sponsoring Committee. For consistency, this group of mostly ordained men will be referred to as the Committee or the Sponsoring Committee until 1965 when it was reorganized as the Brotherly Aid Board. During this time, the appointments to this committee for an unspecified length of time were made by the Bishop Board of the Lancaster Mennonite Conference.

Vine Street Mennonite Church

Galen B. Hostetter was deacon at the Hershey Mennonite Church, also the home congregation of Lloyd Hershey, son of Henry Hershey. To Lloyd and the other officers of the Mennonite Mutual Fire Insurance Company, this new plan would look like a clear invasion of turf. Lloyd wondered why his deacon supported it. And he started asking others.

Many people appreciated Lloyd at Hershey and did their business with him. Galen felt pressure from the people who resented the idea of a new plan and resigned from the committee November 28, 1949, at the end of its 11th meeting at Vine Street.

For the 14 months from October 13, 1948 to November 1949, this conscientious group of deacons, ministers, bishops, and one layman called the Vine Street meetinghouse their home. They held 12 meetings at Vine Street. In addition, they held two other meetings: a meeting at Krady's home in Lyndon, Pennsylvania, to clear the air with Goodville (which had been founded in Goodville, Pennsylvania for auto insurance) and Mennonite Mutual of Intercourse, and an open meeting at the Rohrerstown Mennonite Church, arranged by Andrew Shaub. Andrew felt comfortable having the meeting at Rohrerstown, since his bishop, Christian K. Lehman, was not one to try to stop a good thing.

David Z. Weaver, the lone lay member of the founding team, was a transplant from the Weaverland Mennonite Conference (Horning). In 1942, he had heard a Bible radio program on Seventh-Day Adventist teaching and felt confused. Still confused the next Sunday morning, he and his wife went to the Indiantown Mennonite Church, where Elmer G. Martin was visiting relatives. Elmer was led to preach on the very subject causing conflict in his mind. As David remembers many years later, it was Elmer's sermon that kept him in the Mennonite church.[25]

While in the Horning church David had participated in a church fire plan for his property. By early 1946, David had moved to a farm near the Shirksville church, where he and his wife transferred their membership. Now, on a new farm and in Lancaster Conference, David talked to his bishop, Simon Bucher. "Why don't we have a plan?" he urgently asked Simon. "Even the small Horning group does. You don't need some fancy office or anything. Just the church knows about it."

It struck Simon that someone from an Old Order church coming to Lancaster Conference would have to get commercial insurance because of switching conferences. Simon had been an elder in the Church of the Brethren before transferring to Lancaster Conference. When talk arose of a plan, Simon went to the Byerland meeting ready to tell Stoner and Elmer to press ahead, an encouragement that Stoner did not forget. When the study committee needed another member, Stoner remembered the vivid concern of David, and was glad to suggest Simon Bucher, especially since he represented a new geographic area.

David and Ida Weaver

Information from other plans

At its second meeting the committee decided to get information on other Mennonite plans. Isaac King was asked to get the counsel of John D. Risser, who ran the Hagerstown plan. Stoner Krady was to investigate further the Franconia plan when he went to the area in December. Isaac and Galen Hostetter were to investigate the Morgantown and Old Order Amish plans. Elmer Martin and David Weaver were to go to Belleville, Pennsylvania. David lived close to Lebanon, Pennsylvania and would have a head start on the journey to Belleville.

To carry out the Belleville assignment, Elmer drove in late November to David's house near Frederick, Pennsylvania and parked beside David's garage. David drove his pre-war '39 Chevy to Belleville. The heater of a '39 Chevy was sufficient to warm passengers in the front seat. In the back, people often covered their legs with wool comforters in winter.

Each of the emissary groups took along an 11-point list of questions to explore (typed out and multiplied by carbon paper).[26] The questions were:

- In place of policies what do you give?

- What precautions need to be taken to avoid being forced to take out a charter?

- Do you take into your plan anyone of another church group?

- How do you face the collateral question? What has been your experience?

- How about taking care of storm losses? If not, why not?

- What course do you pursue in cases where either husband or wife is not a church member?

- When there is a loss, what is your procedure to take care of it?

- Do you take into your plan anyone who carries regular insurance?

- Do you list properties and pay losses at full value or only three-fourths? Why?

- How do you take care of a situation where a participant loses church membership?

• How about including automobiles in your plan?

From this list one can almost deduce the first constitution of the proposed plan the committee brought to the bishops.

After driving for several miles David asked Elmer if he remembered preaching at Indiantown six years earlier.

"Oh, yes."

"Do you remember what you preached about?"

"Why, no, I don't believe I do."

David told of the grounding in doctrine Elmer had given him. Committee work was not just business for the church but sometimes personal blessing for individuals.

Bucher Helps the Team

Armed with plenty of data from these investigations, the next tasks were decided and assigned. Elmer was given the first writing assignment for Brotherly Aid on January 10, 1949—an article for the *Pastoral Messenger* to stir up conviction and interest for sharing burdens. The secretary wrote a constitution to present to the Bishop Board.

By January 31, the Bishop Board had given its feedback. Some bishops strongly favored the proposed plan. Some raised questions. By this time David Weaver sensed that the committee was losing direction, floundering about with only test proposals.

Stoner was feeling a loss of momentum too. He recalled Simon's encouraging words and his brilliant stroke of getting David Weaver onto the committee. Stoner asked Simon himself to join the team.

According to David's memory, Simon's coming set the wheels turning again. When he joined the team in February, knowing the bishops' concerns, he advised that they just rewrite the constitution to meet people's concerns. "If this doesn't pass the bishops, how will it pass on the conference floor, where people with strong opinions have almost unlimited power to speak and evoke emotional responses just before a vote?" Simon counseled the stymied committee. "Forget the conference floor and pass it by the bishops. But be quiet about it; let it sell itself. If it works on its own merits it will go." This shrewd advice by Simon turned things around and gave a needed focus.

Clearing the Air With Goodville and Mennonite Mutual Fire

Galen Hostetter knew that most of his fellow farmers in the Hershey congregation were insured with Mennonite Mutual Fire Insurance Association. Proposing an alternative plan made him uneasy. Lloyd Hershey questioned having "two Mennonite companies." Out of courtesy to the folks

"Krady Hollow," the home of Stoner and Frances Krady

at Mennonite Mutual Fire, shouldn't they clear the air with them? he asked the team.

Krady agreed, and the committee set up the next meeting at his home for late April 1949 with representatives from Goodville Mutual and Mennonite Mutual Fire.

As the meeting time approached, Frances Krady was feeling both a bit of anticipation and much nervousness. She was used to getting the home ready for guests. But when others provide your house, you may feel people are watching with just a little more than ordinary interest how you handle it. All her life she and Stoner had lived in houses that they hadn't owned: as a girl, of course, in her parents' house at Bainbridge, Pennsylvania, and then in her sister's house near Mount Joy. After marriage to Stoner, in a farmer's house at EMS, then at the Vine Street mission, and now at the house south of Lancaster.[27]

Stoner often hosted committees he was part of since his house was church property. But the guests at this meeting were not people from the New Danville cluster, or even all ministers, but three insurance men. That set up a tingle of apprehension from what sounded like money and power to Frances. She likely felt some fear because Stoner so often—both in the hearing of his children and from the pulpit—spoke forthrightly against insurance.

Frances was a strong partner in their ministry. Since he was not good at spelling, she, who had more schooling, helped him write his notes for sermons.

That morning as he fed the chickens and goats and helped the children do their chores, Stoner was pondering the irony that insurance men, Mennonite insurance men (almost an oxymoron to him), were invited guests at his house. Well, not his house exactly. Being honest with himself, as he checked the onion sets in the garden, he had never owned property so he really couldn't put himself in their shoes. He glanced at the eaves of the house. Who knows? Maybe secular insurance protected the very roof over his head. If people in his district such as David Newswanger and David Thomas worked so closely with the New Danville Fire Company, who knows what their attitude was about fire insurance.

The Lancaster Conference Rules and Discipline that he had on bended knees agreed to support had been specific only on life insurance. The bishops allowed no deviation from that. But the bishops recognized there were two minds on other kinds of insurance.

Stoner threw some grain to the chickens and resolved to listen more than speak this afternoon.

By 1:30, after lunch, his house was surrounded by black, mostly pre-war cars (no civilian cars were made from 1943 to 1945). The 1946 models looked much like the '42s, a visual testimony of the effects of war that had dedicated metal to be thrown at the enemy. Even the pennies in his pocket were testimony to the war, nickel instead of copper. Now pennies were back to yellow-brown again and people's spirits were picking up, the world becoming ever more enticing to the church.

Even though it was a weekday, Stoner still dressed in his suit, as did the other men. Galen, David, James, Elmer, Andrew, Isaac, and he sat together in his study, almost symbolic of their unity. He was glad David had arrived even though he had the farthest to drive. He came from Lebanon on Route 72, a wide state highway of two full lanes and no stop signs. David, the layman of the committee, although he was only 27 years old, gave the insurance men—none of whom were ordained—the assurance that they were not being grilled by some ecclesiastical court. To further tip the balance of power to the laymen, he would ask one of them to lead the opening prayer.

Ira Hess and Lloyd Hershey of the Mennonite Mutual Fire Insurance Association sat close to the family buffet that had followed the Kradys from the Vine Street residence. Wayne S. Martin sat next to them, representing Goodville Mutual Insurance Company.

Galen Hostetter nodded a nervous greeting to Lloyd Hershey. He didn't think Lloyd was kindly disposed to his serving on this committee, but he would wait and see.

Stoner began the meeting by welcoming everyone to his home. He explained why this meeting was called—"So that we may have an understanding and also avoid any offended feelings." It seemed a home was the right place to feel relaxed. He called on Ira Hess (no relation of James) to lead in prayer.

Then, Ira Hess and Lloyd Hershey took a turn describing their company. It had its origin about 1880, they recalled. Lloyd had taken over the work from his father, Henry. In 1893 the company was reorganized and chartered. They still felt good about carrying Mennonite in their name. "It's a shame," Ira went on, "and I always felt sorry that the Bishop Board did not keep control of the Mennonite Mutual Fire Insurance Association back in 1896 despite the misuse of funds scandal."[28]

Stoner didn't know what scandal Ira was referring to. In 1896, Stoner was only two years old. He glanced at Elmer who also was two years old when the money disappeared. Stoner and Elmer could understand why the bishops chose to distance themselves from a money scandal and turn the company over to the people involved in order to spare the church any litigation.

Wayne Martin of the Goodville Company, located at his home in Goodville, Pennsylvania, said that he had "always felt a mutual plan should be used in the church." "I expressed my conviction," he said, glancing at Elmer, the bishop who was born in his area of Spring Grove, "to three successive bishops in my district and each one turned down the idea." Elmer looked at Stoner.

Lloyd spoke, not daring to catch Deacon Hostetter's eyes: "Just what impression will two organizations within our conference make? Franconia and Virginia each have one plan."

"Well," David Weaver offered, "would you brothers be willing to drop the objectionable features of your organizations and come under conference?" Then we would drop this whole idea of founding a church plan, he implied.

There was silence. Only the sound of robins along the Mill Creek disturbed the room. Ira, Lloyd, and Wayne looked at each other and cleared their throats. Sensing that David's youthful self-confidence might not be the sentiment of the entire group, and not wishing for a stand-off, they merely said that "perhaps, but some things must be considered before that could be done." The idea of "under conference" made them hesitate.

"But what is wrong with the way things are right now?" Ira Hess wondered, making an appeal to the status quo.

Elmer didn't like the tone of David's question about coming under conference but knew that here was the rub: If the "way things are" was right, what case did they have? "Would there be offense on your part," he said kindly to them, "if it seemed right to the conference to go ahead and put this plan into operation?" Both said they would not be offended.

James H. Hess

Elmer's question was honest, because by "conference" he surely meant the Bishop Board. Even though the committee had unanimously agreed to bypass conference and go for the bishops' approval, it had not yet received that.

Everyone agreed that a good spirit prevailed during the afternoon by the Mill Creek. As they shared good wishes around the living room circle, they knew that they could leave in peace assured that the meeting was worthwhile. James Hess led the closing prayer. The fact that this meeting between organizations took place and ended with a good spirit foreshadowed a significant aspect of the way the Brotherly Aid organization functioned throughout its history. Good relationships in the church and between organizations were always important.

Despite the good spirit at the meeting, however, Galen would continue to feel uncomfortable in his congregation. And even though his bishop, Parke Book, would have had no reason to try to stop Galen's serving on the committee, by November Galen would resign from pressure he felt was "stirred up in his district."

While 1949 is now perceived to be a time when ordained people stated the terms of church life to lay people, Galen's resignation is a case of lay people pressuring the ordained. As far as the records show, neither the committee nor anyone associated with the effort to develop a church plan expressed any ill will toward Galen. From the beginning, an attitude of openness and understanding characterized how Brotherly Aid responded toward those who chose not to participate.

As Frances invited the guests to take refreshment in the dining room, the committee took relief in having mended their fences with the players already in the field. Stoner, who had his eye on getting as many people as possible involved, asked whether he shouldn't send copies of the Plan to members of the mission board executive committee. (He wanted Orie Miller to feel included, and he wanted to have the blessing of another powerful lay voice, John H. Mellinger.) Stoner knew the ball game isn't over until the last inning is over, even though you hit a home run in the sixth inning. The committee, over coffee cups, nodded and walked out on the porch to admire the splendid riverside view from Krady's house and the bridge.

Spring onions had already come and gone. People were watching the peas blossom and grow and the sour cherries ripen when the committee met again back at Vine Street.

Galen had recovered from the tension of having been in a meeting with Lloyd and felt free to offer the opening prayer.

Krady reported his experience of testing the plan with mission board members and of finding no obstacles there. It was high time for promotion.

Although there was no budget, and postage was three cents per envelope, they agreed to spend the sum of $7.32 to mail copies of the plan to all 244 ordained members of conference, each lay member of the mission board, and to "a list of lay brethren that was made up by the committee." The committee sensed the importance of involving lay people in this process. It was as though the concept of sharing was influencing the very way that the process developed and enabled those working on the committee to go beyond barriers they otherwise would not have crossed.

All agreed to promote the Plan and pray that Elmer and Stoner would urge the Bishop Board to approve the Plan. Krady had the closing prayer, feeling like the bishops would understand and pass this Plan. The ball was rolling that evening at Vine Street as the members adjourned and walked onto the street full of the sounds of trolleys and industry, the smells of tobacco warehouses, and the wail of steam locomotives in the distance.

— Chapter 5 —

Bishop Board Endorses The Plan

Amos Horst Hosts the Bishops

The sun beat down on the roof of the Indiantown Mennonite Church. By 1:00 p.m., the day of July 28, 1949 was already warm. The newspaper predicted it would get hot.[29] Bishop Amos Horst was at home in his Hammer Creek district of 1,315 members in nine congregations.

Concerned about the guests' comfort, Amos glanced around Indiantown to see if he had pulled down all the upper windows. The frames were still good even though the building was erected in 1819. He hoped the building would stay the way it was, and he hoped the conference would not change too much during his tenure.

Amos's district stretched from Landis Valley (where Minister Ira D. Landis was conservative in some ways but advocating for a historical society) to Myerstown and Ephrata (where Minister Mahlon Zimmerman would rise up to become his assistant and successor). Among the members in his district was the well-known and old evangelist, John S. Hess.

This district was mostly conservative, but it had its people to watch. At Ephrata one of the sheep of the fold, Orie O. Miller, traveled the world, exerted uncanny force in mission board and Mennonite Central Committee circles, and kept working on a seemingly endless series of new organizations, such as the suspect Mennonite Mutual Aid. At Amos's urging in 1950, Orie would send a letter of apology to the Bishop Board for having sent a mailing about Mennonite Mutual Aid to the Lancaster Conference constituency.

Amos Horst

If that were not enough to keep Amos alert to insurrection, at Lititz he had to keep a sharp eye on the youthful Howard H. Charles, who seemed to be dreaming of wider horizons and asking about higher education. Had he heard that Howard had inquired about studying at Goshen Biblical Seminary in Indiana? Amos shrugged off the suspicion.

Bishops Arrive

Amos greeted each of his fellow bishops at Indiantown Mennonite Church with a holy kiss. He was proud to welcome them to his district. But being the host put an edge of responsibility on his shoulders today.

As the bishops arrived Amos informally counted them. Christian K. Lehman of the Manor area was warm to him. If not a stickler for the Rules and Discipline that were constantly under fire, he was an open and accepting person. Noah Risser had come on the early side, probably fearing he would have to take leadership if W. W. Graybill, conference moderator, failed to grasp something.

Noah Mack and Richard Danner had a long drive from York and Hanover. While tires did not blow out as often as they did during the war, you could count on radiators of six-cylinder Chevies heating up on hills.

Henry Lutz arrived on time in his Chrysler. J. Paul Graybill, soon to turn 50 years old, arrived with a youthful step and the bearing of the man of the moment, but careful not to give evidence of any liberal leanings. He was bishop of the largest district in the conference and the principal of Lancaster Mennonite School. Although his car bespoke no special rank, his bearing and his bespectacled eyes did.

John Kennel, Parke Book, Jacob Harnish, and Simon Bucher walked into Indiantown. Bucher was the Brethren boy who claimed he accepted Lancaster Conference rules because conference made "its rules to please God, not man." In 1968, when the rules had changed too much, he placed his lot with the new and more conservative "Eastern" group.

Amos got the warmest handshake and holy kiss from D. Stoner Krady, who met people with a smile, as though being a bishop did not diminish his enjoyment of life one whit. Finally Elmer Martin arrived. He had spent the morning tending to business at Ezra W. Martin Company, a meatpacking concern.

Still the moderator did not arrive.

While they waited a few minutes and enjoyed conversation, a visiting bishop arrived. Amos had almost forgotten his name. Stanley Beidler came by invitation to speak to an agenda item concerning a minister in the Franconia Conference. Beidler's trip from Harleysville was a good reason to hold the meeting at Indiantown. Of course, he traveled by state roads, since the "dream highway," the Pennsylvania Turnpike, was still under construction.

The Meeting Begins

Amos waited a moment longer. Moderator W. W. Graybill still did not arrive. His 44 years of service as bishop and his advanced age were taking a toll on him, Amos noticed from meeting to meeting. Never mind the driving from Juniata County.

Around the edges some bishops mentioned the matter of succession. When that would become an issue, they whispered that the custom of seniority might be hard to apply. Noah Risser, second in seniority, was quite old and didn't seem eager to take the mantle of moderator of the Bishop Board and of conference.

Amos Horst, who would be elected secretary of conference at the Bishop Board meeting in one month, looked around the circle of plain-coated bishops. He glanced at Henry Lutz, who had been the secretary until March this past year, and he gave him the nod to go ahead. The youngest ones already had their jackets off, and their sleeve garters looked tight in the waves of July heat.

Hosting the bishop board meeting was enough for Amos Horst. He had his share of chairing meetings with the Mennonite Bible School board of Lancaster Conference. The five-member board was easier to handle than these

Pennsylvania Turnpike

sixteen bishops. Some members of the Bible school board were J. Paul Graybill, Simon Bucher, and John R. Kraybill, who was the treasurer (an office that the Bishop Board didn't have yet).

Also on the school board was a young minister from far south on Route 222, James H. Hess. He was impressing Amos with his commitment to church institutions. "Go make ready a people prepared for the Lord" (Luke 1:17) was the motto of the fledgling Bible school. That might have summed up the mentality of Lancaster Conference in 1949.

In just months the 20th century would begin its second half. And some things would change. Today this 15-member group of bishops would weigh in the balances one of those 1950 changes, a plan for brotherly aid.

Elmer Martin and Stoner Krady exchanged glances: this would be the meeting to ask for permission to proceed with the plan. But at Indiantown this quiet July 1949, brotherly aid wasn't even on the agenda—yet.

The guest from Franconia was responding to a request to the Bally-Boyertown congregation to ordain George Miller of Bally, Pennsylvania, who with his wife, Sister Grace, was appointed for mission work in Honduras. Stoner sat up a bit taller, since it was in his Lancaster district that Central American work began.

Bishop Beidler read the response from the Franconia Conference, which had not yet committed itself to foreign mission work. He read: They appreciated the conviction that George has for foreign mission work, but when it comes to ordaining him, the bench in his congregation is not in unity on the value of mission work. So they suggested George and Grace transfer membership to a Lancaster Conference congregation.

Which congregation would do that? Noah Risser asked.

"Vine Street," Stoner ventured.

The bishops approved, and Beidler left.

Finding leadership in Cumberland County and Alabama was considered next. Institutional building required new ways to call leaders. The group acted to give permission to the Placement Committee to call experienced lay brethren as workers. Elmer Martin took note and nodded.

He, Parke Book, and J. Paul Graybill comprised that committee to find mission workers and to screen them. J. Paul himself came to leadership through mission work in Philadelphia. Stoner Krady, too, came to ordination through a mission institution.

Brotherly Aid Plan Approved

Now Stoner Krady spoke again, asking permission to introduce an agenda item that had already been worked on pretty carefully. He and Elmer Martin, he said, would like a green light to go ahead with a brotherly aid plan "for fire, storm, and wind." This was not the first time this duo brought the Bishop

Board up to date on the proposed brotherly aid plan. On January 28, 1949, it was introduced by a letter written by the secretary, James H. Hess.

By this time, the bishops were assured that this was neither the "western" (Goshen, Indiana) mutual aid sneaking its nose under the Lancaster tent nor insurance masquerading as piety.[30] In fact, Stoner was often heard to speak against insurance. People weren't quite so sure about Elmer, with his large investments in the Martin meat company. Stoner's and Elmer's update assured them that church buildings would not be assessed, that no unequal yoke would be broached.

Noah Risser, whose own insurance needs might have been considerable, allowed anyone who had comments to speak. Then it was "moved and supported that the committee appointed by the executive board of conference to develop a brotherly aid plan," Amos jotted quickly and precisely, "also be permitted to operate the plan as presented."

"Permitted to operate the plan."

That decision threw the switch. But no one moved.

At Indiantown, fifteen men opened the final gate for Brotherly Aid to come off the trial track and before the people. A small step for the Bishop Board. A large step awaited the 13,500 members of the Lancaster Conference congregations.

In less than a month, on August 22, Stoner would announce this Bishop Board action to the full Brotherly Aid committee. "This action by the Bishop Board was unanimously accepted by our committee," read the minutes.

Timing of the Approval

Why did this plan pass muster with the church in 1949 when Orie Miller's 1939 plan didn't? A few hints appear between the lines. Even though the bishops were substantially the same group of men in 1939 as in 1949, the times were different. This plan came into being after World War II. In the air was a feeling that the church can and should build institutions.

"A home for mentally ill" was already appearing in the Bishop Board minutes. In April 1949 Mr. and Mrs. Graybill Landis gave their Mt. Gretna farm for that purpose. Lancaster Mennonite School was in its seventh year. Talk of having a Lancaster Conference farm for the children of missionaries was debated. Some conservative-minded leaders urged that Lancaster Conference be a self-sufficient denomination so that western-based progressive influences, including Mennonite Mutual Aid, would not tempt people.

Already the bishops were having strained discussions with O. N. Johns of Ohio, who was shepherding impatient or liberal souls in Lancaster Conference who wanted fewer rules and discipline.

Since 1939, a scriptural foundation for mutual aid had been laid by J. Winfield Fretz and others, such as the Hesses at Byerland, who could understand that new forms of mutual aid would be needed. Orie had gotten the administrative mechanics ahead of the cultural, religious story.

The plan approved in 1949 started in the right place, with the right actors. No matter how strong conference may have been in forcing the hand of congregations in some areas, it never forgot that the constituent blocks of the whole organization were the congregations and districts. And when the New Danville cluster made a simple request to establish a systematic plan to share property losses, there was no reason to stop the home-grown convictions, nourished though they had been by churchwide showers of theological rain.

The actors were right, too. Look at the bishops already part of the plan committee: Krady and Martin, in the late '40s definitely two of the most active on the board. Nauman was not going to fight this with his whole district and bishop behind it.

Amos Horst would probably come along, as ten years ago he had presented Orie's plan for the mission board, although he would resist Mennonite Mutual Aid for some more years. Henry Lutz, who had gone to all the trouble to record the lost proposal in 1939, was bound to support it this time, too. Simon Bucher had given his benediction at the Byerland meeting and had made his full support known.

Right on the inside of the action were these six bishops, mostly significant voices. Six out of 16 was more than one-third. J. Paul Graybill knew the school board of Lancaster Mennonite School had some construction plans in mind and would rather have Lancaster Conference coverage than another company. The bishops promoting Philhaven (the "home for mentally handicapped") had construction in mind, too, having just recently acquired the Landis farm and needing to consider coverage. That brought to half the number of the bishops who would outright support the plan.

The voices who might oppose were Danner and Bomberger. Both of them (along with Bucher, just a year or two before his death) would eventually leave the Conference to form separate groups.

So although Brotherly Aid did not have a petition signed by 15 leaders as Lancaster Mennonite School had had in 1940, it had an even stronger germination—an exploratory district-sponsored meeting, endorsed by surrounding leaders in Franconia, the Amish of Morgantown, and the Mennonites of Hagerstown. With a cast of such salt-of-the-earth spectators watching, who would mount an opposing faction and why? Bomberger did join the Plan, and by 1967 he had received from it.

So in 1949 any anti-institution leaders had little voice to stop it. Any doctrinal purists had no case to make, with all the scripture quoting on the side of the plan. Any liberals who thought the conference should join another group's plan had nothing to point to. The Mennonite Mutual Fire Insurance Association in Intercourse was a public company since its founding and unfortunate disinheriting by the church leaders a full half century earlier.

About the only other path of resistance to Brotherly Aid was the "trust only in the Lord" rhetoric that was still coming from the pen of a few leaders such as John L. Stauffer, but people viewed this as one part of the answer, not the full answer.

With all the ground work laid by Krady and the committee, it is hard to imagine the Bishop Board in July 1949 saying "No."

This Plan also worked unlike the 1939 proposal by Orie Miller because it did not implicate the bishops in any legalities or increase their workload. It succeeded because it was quiet in a decade of loud voices. It kept a polite and discreet distance. It succeeded because Krady, its founding chair, got people involved and connected.

At Indiantown the administrative approval was totally cleared. Now the members of the committee could run the rest of the home stretch with a benediction on their heads.

Indiantown Mennonite Church
where the Bishop Board gave the green light to establish
a brotherly aid plan in 1949

— Chapter 6 —

Fire and Storm Plan Gets Established

Context of Fire and Storm's Founding

If April 1, 1950 was remembered for anything, besides the inane jokes credited to April Fools' Day, it was for the first day of the decennial U.S. census. The head-counter that year counted 150,697,361 people living in the United States. The Mennonite head-counters that year tallied 14,061 Mennonites in Lancaster Conference. The *Mennonite Yearbook* accounted for 67,399 in the U.S. and Canada.[31]

Carl and Mary Weaver were owners of this farm in 1950, the first farm to be covered by the Brotherly Aid Fire and Storm Plan on April 1, 1950.

John D. Risser who ran the Hagerstown mutual aid plan in the 1940s gave counsel for starting the Brotherly Aid Fire and Storm Plan.

But in the minds of the Brotherly Aid members, April 1, 1950 was the day they became responsible in the mutual guardianship of $1 million in property. That $1 million included the farm of Carl and Mary Weaver of Elm, Pennsylvania, the first to sign an agreement.

On February 1, 1950, the Safety Responsibility Act of Pennsylvania became the law of the Commonwealth. Forty-two other states (of the 48) had similar laws requiring reporting and deposits for accidents. If you read the newspapers and listened to the radio, you knew something regarding auto liability would change. It was little wonder that a few people at the Mellinger meeting in 1949 urged that autos be considered in the property plan.

Newspapers kept people abreast of the highway tragedies. On April 1, 1950, the day Fire and Storm went into operation, the Lancaster *Intelligencer Journal* noted briefly that Harold and Miriam Meyer and "a Mountain Top (Pennsylvania) man escaped with slight injuries" in a head-on collision. Harold suffered "abrasions of the right wrist and both knees and lacerations of the nose and chin," while Miriam had bruises on the right ankle and the right knee and also lacerations to the knee. Beside the article, strategically placed on the page, was a small ad for auto insurance. "Your local Harleysville agent" was identified as Clayton R. Leaman.

Newspapers graphically covered fires. In the same April 1 issue, a three-line article with a Reading Associated Press dateline stated that "two infants died in a fire which swept their home."

Sponsoring Committee Fades Into Background

Once the Brotherly Aid Sponsoring Committee had given birth to the sharing plan, the committee itself went into eclipse. The records show that after March 28, 1950, it did not meet formally again until October 5, 1953.[32] Krady, Martin, Bucher, and the secretarial pen of James Hess, of course, would meet at semiannual conference meetings and mission board settings. And of course they planned and executed the annual meeting of Brotherly Aid. But they had confidence that the operation of the Plan was in the good hands of the operating committee: Clarence Harnish, Andrew Shaub, and Roy Ulrich.

Krady, Martin, and Bucher, the three bishops of the Brotherly Aid committee, had many more things to occupy their minds after April 1.

Stoner Krady, the personable, smiling chair, would get mission work in Honduras off to a soaring start, including a visit there. Elmer Martin, keeping his position as manager of the meat business, was given many conference assignments. Simon Bucher's star in the conference was still rising. James Hess, too, was appointed to numerous assignments.

Meanwhile, Roy, Andrew, and Clarence juggled their many assignments at Millwood Mennonite Church, Rohrerstown, and Willow Street, respectively. Local committees did the actual site visitation and writing of agreements.

Clarence Harnish Appointed Chair

For Clarence H. Harnish, church work in addition to farming ran in the family. He had learned it from an early age, being the oldest son of Bishop Jacob T. Harnish. When Jacob retired from farming in 1942, he settled in Lyndon, near the home Stoner Krady occupied from 1938 to 1959. For 27 years he was chair of the board of Oreville Mennonite Home, now Mennonite Home.

In 1950, Clarence was living on the Willow Street farm with five children, the oldest 19, the youngest 8. Clarence served as chair of the Brotherly Aid Fire and Storm Plan until 1973. It is likely he attended the 1948 New Danville district meeting, for in the July 1950 issue of the *Pastoral Messenger*, the editor, J. Paul Graybill, ran a 26-line announcement of the plan below a spacious two-column head. The article, attributed to Clarence, declared that "the plan is now available whereby brethren of the Lancaster Mennonite Conference area may systematically help bear one another's burdens in relation to loss by fire, storm, or lightning, of building and contents."

The "systematic" phrase surely came from the Risser remark at Byerland two years earlier. The notice goes on, lifting from the constitution another phrase: "This organization has been effected by permission of and subject to the executive board of Lancaster Conference."

First Fire and Storm Committee
(Left to right): Clarence Harnish, chair; Andrew Shaub, treasurer;
and Roy Ulrich, secretary

That is word for word from the Brotherly Aid constitution of 1950. It states from the beginning that Brotherly Aid was part of Lancaster Conference, not just tolerated by it.

Ulrich and Shaub

Roy Ulrich, the first secretary of the Brotherly Aid General Committee, which operated the Plan, was born August 19, 1909, the son of Andrew B. Ulrich and Ella Unzicker. He was baptized by Joseph Reber of Shelbyville, Illinois. On June 22, 1946, he was married to Rebecca Riehl by Bishop John A. Stoltzfus at the Weavertown Beachy Amish Church, Bird-in-Hand, Pennsylvania. On December 18, 1957, Bishop LeRoy S. Stoltzfus ordained him as minister at Millwood Mennonite Church. Winfield Ruth preached. Twelve years later, in 1969, he withdrew from Lancaster Conference to join the Eastern group.

The youngest of the trio operating the Plan when it went into effect was Andrew Shaub, born December 7, 1919. He was also the link between the Brotherly Aid Committee and the Plan itself. The son of C. Newton and

Lydia G. Hertzler, he was baptized January 31, 1932 at Rohrerstown by John H. Moseman. On June 14, 1941, he was married to Ruth Mae (Charles), one year his junior, by Bishop Christian K. Lehman. By July 16, 1946, only months before his 25th birthday, he was ordained a deacon for Rohrerstown. Andrew was with Brotherly Aid in some capacity from 1949 until 1990. After that he served for a while as janitor of the office building.

First Brotherly Aid Annual Meeting

At 1:00 p.m. Tuesday, November 14, 1950, the Brotherly Aid Plan held its first annual meeting, as called for by the constitution, at the Elizabethtown Mennonite Church. For the first time since the New Danville annual congregational meeting, Stoner Krady did not chair a Brotherly Aid meeting. Stoner asked Clarence Lutz to do that, since he was the minister at that congregation. Stoner was there, of course, and led in the closing prayer.

After the Plan began, the operating committee (known as the General Committee)—Harnish, Shaub, and Ulrich—moved to center stage. Reports were given by the chair, Clarence, and the treasurer, Andrew Shaub. Curiously, Frank Enck, a minister who took Stoner's place at Vine Street, was the auditor, since there had been no previous annual meeting at which to elect auditors. It is likely Stoner just tapped someone close to him. The first annual meeting began with J. Paul Graybill, the editor of the *Pastoral Messenger* and the principal of Lancaster Mennonite School, preaching on "Scriptural Principles for Brotherly Aid." That was preceded by the "short sermon," or devotions, by John A. Kennel, the bishop of Roy Ulrich.

John D. Risser, who had been at the 1948 meeting, addressed the topic, "In the Light of Past Experience What Does Brotherly Aid Offer for the Future?" Brother Risser operated the Hagerstown plan, and again he noted that Brotherly Aid is a "systematic way for caring for others." He said that Brotherly Aid offers a "uniform, satisfactory, and economical" way to do that.

The final item on the program was an open discussion. Several people spoke and raised these issues:

- What is the tax status of Brotherly Aid?

- Why not trust God instead of having a plan?

- Could this organization get too large?

- What if a brother asks for help when he isn't in need?

- Will buildings be covered while being built?

A typical farm in 1950
such as the one pictured above was valued at about $25,000.

• Does Brotherly Aid offer general liability?

Number 3 was not surprising, given the astonishing treasurer's report of just an hour earlier. Andrew Shaub had matter-of-factly, but distinctly, read the amount of valuation covered as of October 31, 1950. Just seven short months since operation began, just a year since the Mellinger meeting when it looked like $900,000 had been committed—Andrew reported a figure in seven figures: $3,641,270. That figure, in 1950 dollars, could ring bells of alarm to farmers whose barns were selling for about $30,000, and whose houses were worth about $10,000. Too big, indeed! If in the millions already, could it reach a billion by the 45th anniversary?

Second Annual Meeting

While the first annual meeting went west to Elizabethtown, the second annual meeting on November 13, 1951 was back to the roots. This one was held at the New Danville meetinghouse, again on Tuesday afternoon. Parke Book moderated the proceedings. LeRoy Stoltzfus, the widely traveled bishop from Millwood, and Noah Risser of the Elizabethtown district had devotions and prayer. Then Bishop Simon Bucher spoke on "Brotherly Aid versus Insurance." Premiums to insurance, Bucher said, promote "too much of the unequal yoke, help pay high salaries of the insurance people, and help to build up a large reserve fund."

At the second annual meeting, "back to the roots" was also the rally cry for a plan of promotion. The Brotherly Aid Committee already faced the issue of publicity several times. Now a new face, a firm believer in Brotherly Aid, Edwin H. Gehman, enthusiastically suggested ways to promote Brotherly Aid at the grass roots. Local committee members "need to be sold on the plan" and have a knowledge of it, he told them. When someone complains about insurance costing too much, the local committee person has "a wonderful opportunity to promote Brotherly Aid."

While the first year emphasized the operating committee, the theme of the second annual meeting might have been "the local committee." A roll call of local committee members followed. Of the 30 on the roll, a full 21 were present, and they received instructions.[33]

Andrew Shaub gave not only the treasurer's report (valuation at $8.25 million, more than double the first report) but also the third message based on Psalm 116:6, "The Lord hath done great things for us, whereof we are glad."

At the end of the meeting a man who raised chickens asked how to set the valuation on his flock, since the value grew by the week.

Then there were prayers that "God would lead and direct all that they undertake or do, and if this be not according to God's will that He bring it to naught."

Neither Parke nor Stoner knew what the Manheim district bishop might think of Brotherly Aid. But since Homer Bomberger was in the meeting, he was asked to lead the closing prayer. This bridge-building in the Bishop Board was almost complete with Homer's blessing.

Third Annual Meeting

For the third meeting, November 11, 1952, Simon Bucher remembered his conversation with David Z. Weaver and invited the annual meeting to the Gingrich meetinghouse. By this meeting the roll call of committee members got onto the printed program. "Round table discussions" became the watchword to process the concerns of the group. Less time was given to a series of speakers and more time to operational information. The roll call showed that 25 of the 36 representatives were present.

James Hess, who five years earlier helped found this Plan, which in 1952 already covered almost $12.5 million in valuations, spoke on the "Faithfulness of Our Lord." While James made clear that Christians could trust God's faithfulness, Walter Shank asked for ten minutes to speak about the faithfulness, or lack thereof, of the brethren of the Plan. He related a few losses that a change in the constitution could cover.

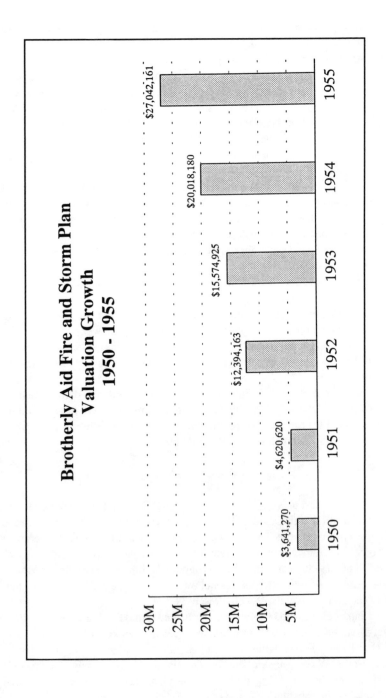

By the third year, Shaub, Harnish, and Ulrich must have wondered how they could deal with all the complicated cases. During open discussion these questions were raised:

- If a son takes over property from a father, does the initial fee apply?

- If property is sold, can the valuation be transferred?

- Shall we include flood coverage? (Straw vote taken, negative result; discussion at length.)

- Shall young men coming into Plan pay assessment the first year?

This vigorous discussion prompted Bishop Amos Horst to propose that a committee be appointed "to consider if it be necessary to broaden our plan." A brother seconded that thought, suggesting that Lancaster Conference should have one fund for all losses.

Elmer Martin, who was moderating this meeting and perhaps hoping to visit relatives before returning home, looked at Clarence, knowing what lengthy discussion such a question could unleash. When he saw the same concern on the faces of the operating committee, Elmer called for aging Bishop Noah Risser to lead the closing prayer. It had been hard enough to get this simple Plan into operation.

The losses of Arthur Good by fire and Isaac H. Gehman by storm were $2,700 and $2,650, respectively. Twelve other storm, lightning, and fire losses—one for $10—had brought losses to $9,142 that year.

It seemed that things were complicated enough. For now.

A new 1953 Ford Sedan sold for $1,988.00.

— *Chapter 7* —

Liability Plan Begins

Complicated, maybe. But life was complicated and getting more so in 1953. Family life for many middle-class people in 1953 meant one family car, a mortgage on a $12,000 house, and inflation at four percent. The father's job covered all the expenses of the family. The mother's contribution was considerable outside the money economy.

The family car usually meant a trusty Chevy, Ford, or Plymouth. A few of the more daring men bought Oldsmobiles or Buicks. New cars cost about $2,000, almost one-third of a carpenter's annual wages.

In 1953, the Lancaster Mennonite Conference was growing in numbers and activity. Trolleys once shuttled people to can applesauce for old institutions such as the Millersville Children's Home. Now autos were taking Mennonites in droves to tent meetings, to street meetings in Philadelphia and Harrisburg, and to missionary conferences at Lancaster Mennonite School.[34]

As the dangers of World War II receded in memory, new dangers appeared—accidents on the road and subversive politics in America, namely Communists.

It seemed to Senator McCarthy and the many others who made a profession of fearing Communists that life after the war was more dangerous. It seemed to them that an evil in life, even more dangerous than German submarines and idolatrous Nazi ideology, had taken secret abode among American citizens. Everyone was suspect. Innocence had to be proven. Once accused of having Communist sympathies, anyone could instantly become an outcast.

The same tone of fear and mistrust could sometimes be heard in church circles. In the early 1950s hardly a Bishop Board meeting went by without mention of an investigation into someone's complaint about someone else. No one was exempt. Bishops as well as anyone else took their knocks.

In this climate of fear, the roads were no safer a place for retreat. An out-of-state license was sure bait for a small-town policeman looking for easy income for his borough. By 1953, 42,864,000 autos traveled the roads of the U.S., up from 30,499,608 in 1943.[35]

Automobile Insurance Topic of 1950s

The February 1, 1950 Pennsylvania Safety Responsibility Act had prompted a flurry of fear and concern that the new law may force people into a state versus conscience test. After J. Paul Graybill and several Franconia Conference people had met with some state officials, the Bishop Board wrote a letter that was to be read in every congregation. People feared that the new law would require auto liability insurance. The letter noted that "among our brotherhood there are those who have conscientious reasons for not carrying automobile insurance." It went on to note that the new law "does not require insurance," but holds those involved responsible. It urged people to comply with the law requiring reports.

The letter urged people "to be helpful to each other" and "to continue in faith and trust in the Lord and in the Church," and, "since there are different views in the church concerning the insurance question," that we be "mutually helpful to each other when there is need." A fine prologue to the Plan about to be founded, but no mention of it.

Auto Liability Considered

At 2:30 p.m. on October 5, 1953, the school day at Lancaster Mennonite School was winding down under the colorful leaves of the campus. Amos W. Weaver was adjusting quickly to his new job as principal. He had just succeeded J. Paul Graybill, whose decade of service had ended. Taking office just four weeks earlier, Amos had said to the chapel assembly that "the world's on fire with Communistic atheism," a theme of many politicians, too, that fall.[36]

As students walked to their final class of the day, Amos glanced out his window of the administration building. He noticed nine black cars drive onto campus and park near the girls' dormitory. His date book showed no meeting he had to attend. Were these the cars of parents coming early to pick up dorm students for the weekend at home? Dean Noah Good noticed the cars, too. Probably a few board members to pay a surprise visit, Good might have surmised, especially when he noticed the young preacher and Lancaster Mennonite School board secretary, James Hess, get out of his Ford.

Or a friendly visit? As tense as things had become during Graybill's last year, it might be a simple visit to encourage the new principal. When they saw three bishops—Stoner Krady, Simon Bucher, and Elmer Martin—walk toward the new dormitory, they might have feared something serious was afoot, though. They noticed Edwin Gehman, Willis Kling, Peter Smith, Andrew Shaub, and Isaac King. The office secretary likely reminded Weaver and Good of the request to use the lounge for a meeting of Brotherly Aid. Noah got back to correcting German tests.

Lancaster Mennonite High School girls' dormitory
where the first Brotherly Aid Liability Plan meeting was held in 1953

The group meeting in the dormitory lounge quickly had a round of handshakes. Noticing the suitcases packed for the quick weekend getaway around them, they found seats as close as possible to the far corner. James Hess readied his fountain pen and looked over the group around him. There was Peter Smith, a deacon at the Stauffer Mennonite Church, in Clarence Lutz's district around Elizabethtown.

Edwin Gehman had made his interest in Brotherly Aid known. It was certain that he would give time to the cause. Willis E. Kling, a deacon in the Paradise district, was there.

Amos Weaver and Noah Good, who at first thought something was afoot, were right. They were present for the very first meeting in 1953 when the Brotherly Aid Liability Plan was approved. In 1995, forty-two years after the 1953 meeting, this Plan would have 30,000 autos (one-half the number of all the cars in Lancaster County in 1953) and 29,000 drivers. Brotherly Aid's annual budget would dwarf the Lancaster Mennonite High School's budget by the end of three decades.

The group quickly agreed to keep Krady and Hess in their roles of chair and secretary, respectively. Simon Bucher, Elmer Martin, Andrew Shaub, and Isaac King were the sponsoring committee members. The group noted the move of Melvin Kauffman, who had been appointed to this committee, but agreed not to bother finding anyone to take his place. Simon Bucher, aware of his role as assistant conference moderator, consented "to give counsel and advice but desired not to be asked to take the initiative."[37]

Again, James Hess had done his homework by getting copies of Virginia and Washington County conference auto liability plans. Discussion favored setting up an auto plan similar to the Fire and Storm Plan, since it was working so well.

While the group hammered out these decisions, the day students roared out of campus, many of them in uninsured cars. Amos Weaver and Noah Good went home. It was soon milking time, so the group decided to meet in a month at the Oreville Home. But that date and place did not hold, and two weeks later, on November 21, 1953, the committee met at the home of Stoner Krady.

At Krady Hollow, before tackling the auto plan at hand, the group decided on the remuneration to the Brotherly Aid Fire and Storm Plan General Committee for the previous year: Clarence Harnish $176, Roy Ulrich $242, Andrew Shaub $215 (a little less than $1.50 per hour).

Plan Begins to Take Shape

With the $633 payroll taken care of (in 1951 it had been $250), the men turned their attention to the auto plan. James's investigation of the Virginia plan was considered. "The discussion that followed revealed that this committee does not favor a plan such as the Virginia brethren have," noted the minutes.

In the plan that would emerge that day, the committee made these points:

- An advisory council could review all accidents

- The plan would conform to Pennsylvania law of posting money upon an accident (escrow)

- The plan would promote Christian driving behavior (education)

- A card would be given in place of Pennsylvania insurance card

Each committee member was given the homework of studying the original Brotherly Aid Plan constitution before the next meeting in view of how to adapt it for auto liability. The secretary would obtain information "from Harrisburg" regarding financial responsibility of those involved in accidents. The next meeting would be 1:00 p.m. Saturday, January 2, 1954, at Krady Hollow.

But again life's demands postponed the meeting until the afternoon of January 23. James Hess read the Pennsylvania Safety Responsibility Act in its entirety and the group discussed it. Unlike the simplicity of property aid, from the beginning the Brotherly Aid Liability Plan involved the complexity of auto law. The group also reviewed the Brotherly Aid constitution line by line to see what could apply.

The February meeting was delayed one week; the committee finally met in Annville, Pennsylvania, at the home of Simon Bucher. "The entire afternoon was spent in going over...the Brotherly Aid Plan constitution...and adapting it to the auto aid plan."

James agreed to send copies of the adapted constitution to members before the next committee meeting, which would be during the lunch hour of the mission board meeting at Elizabethtown church on March 10.

Temporary Roadblock

A typically lengthy agenda confronted the March 15, 1954 Bishop Board meeting at the East Petersburg meetinghouse. Simon Bucher first focused attention on a proposed revision of the Rules and Discipline. Several hours passed on that issue. Then came a request from Charles Hostetter to put fliers about the Mennonite Hour radio air times in *The Way* when it was distributed by youth groups. The secretary was requested to get further information from Charlie. Another Virginia enterprise, Eastern Mennonite College, came knocking at the door with a request to send appeals to deacons for student aid.

The bishops voted that down. They had not liked Virginia's auto plan either. Stoner remembered his good days at Eastern Mennonite College and squirmed a little at the negative vote. He looked across the room at Christian K. Lehman, who was having his own squirming problem, puzzled as he usually was by a mentality that feared anything not based at home.

The hour was late when Stoner finally presented the "Brotherly Aid plan for auto liability." Responses were weary and mixed. The Bishop Board secretary recorded that the motion to "look favorably upon the movement and recommend that the committee further study implications and report it at a later meeting was lost."[38]

Lost!

Stoner and Elmer were stunned, at least for a moment. Suspect a radio preacher. Suspect Eastern Mennonite College. But a conference-based sharing plan? By now all the bishops had participated in Brotherly Aid meetings. Perhaps Stoner in his optimism and enthusiasm had made the motion sound too much like asking for a blank check.

But whatever the secretary wrote in the minutes was not what Stoner heard and felt. As he pondered the action the secretary wrote, he had a hunch that this roadblock was temporary. It was just part of the machinery of testing the spirits, knowing that once the horse is out of the barn it is useless to try to close the door. When the Bishop Board-appointed Sponsoring

Committee met back at his home May 29, Stoner asked Simon Bucher to present the bishops' reaction.

To Simon, nothing, board minute or no board minute, had changed. He told them that "the plan as it stands at present in its incomplete form met no definite opposition." Yet "the board desired a more complete picture of our plan before they were ready to give a definite word on it." That was hard-knock administrative thinking.

So that spring day the committee moved ahead and made a "few minor changes." A straw vote on a name for the plan followed. "Brotherly Aid Liability for Motor Vehicles" received two votes. It had the sound of a bureau in Harrisburg. The simpler "Brotherly Aid Liability Plan" received five votes. The name Brotherly Aid Liability Plan was born in Lyndon in Stoner Krady's study. At the next meeting on July 10, the committee agreed to include livestock in the liability plan, especially when cows crossed a road from pasture to stable.

After the mission board session at Stumptown July 14, at 5:30 p.m., Stoner exercised his magic again and invited bishops Jacob Harnish, Noah Risser, and Homer Bomberger to join an ad hoc meeting with all members present. They dropped any restrictions for the size of trucks. With six of the sixteen bishops present they decided to present the revised plan again to the Bishop Board.

Seek Liability Plan Personnel

On July 15, 1954, the Bishop Board met at East Petersburg. The bishops gave counsel on an estate settlement and on non-Lancaster Conference speakers at Lancaster Mennonite School, and urged people to be in prayer for the Howard Hammer revival.

Stoner had already led devotions based on Philippians 3. Now he felt confident to present a progress report on the Brotherly Aid Liability Plan. The secretary of conference this time wrote, "agreed to give permission to acquire more information."

It was at this meeting at East Petersburg in July 1954 that the Bishop Board gave the Brotherly Aid Liability Plan administrative consent to form and operate. What was lost in March was regained in July. The key words were "agreed to give permission." In the terse language of Bishop Board minutes, this was the green light.

The Sponsoring Committee met again at Edwin Gehman's home in rural Denver, Pennsylvania on August 21, 1954 at 1:30 p.m. Krady "reported that the bishop board has granted permission to this committee to proceed to put this plan into operation." The air in Denver must have seemed spring-like that heavy summer day.

After Stoner Krady enthusiastically announced Bishop Board consent to continue, James Hess got out the list of candidates to run the Plan. The possible personnel already nominated were Martin Ressler, Harvey Zimmerman, Earl Nissley, Samuel Wenger, and members of the sponsoring committee itself: Edwin Gehman, Willis Kling, and Peter Smith.

The committee now tried to draw up a final list of candidates. From the original list, the committee pruned off Samuel Wenger, Peter Smith, and Willis Kling.

Wenger could give legal counsel for the Plan but would not want to operate it. Besides, he was a board member of Mennonite (Auto) Aid, Inc., of Goshen, Indiana. Smith and Kling bowed out, probably feeling that they had invested enough through these meetings that still were not ended. Lester Wenger of Lititz and Emanuel Martin of Annville were approved and added to the list. Lester, along with Elam Stoner, had audited the conference's books as early as 1948. He looked like a good choice.

It still did not seem as if they had what they needed. The chances were high that some would not accept such a large assignment. Elmer Martin shifted a bit in his seat. Something was coming to his mind.

He had taken notice of a capable man at Stumptown who had a white-collar (underneath his plain coat) office job at Pennsylvania Power and Light Company. He had only one child and no farm and was good at book work—J. Kendig Miller. He also thought of his bookkeeper at Ezra Martin Company—Ivan D. Leaman, a meticulous keeper of figures. Elmer suggested those two men, almost as an afterthought. At the eleventh hour their names were added to the list. The committee invited the candidates and "other interested persons" to a Saturday afternoon September 4 meeting at the Mellinger Mennonite Church.

Every member of the committee except Peter Smith was there, as were the seven curious yet cautious men in plain coats. Martin Ressler, Harvey Zimmerman, and Edwin Gehman had been at the head of the list since it was first drawn up. Lester Wenger and Earl Nissley did not come.

But Emanuel Martin came; and Ivan Leaman and Kendig Miller were interested enough to show up. Roy Ulrich showed up to help plan the program for the fifth annual meeting of Brotherly Aid which was to be held at Paradise.

When Lester Wenger and Earl Nissley declined to serve, Stoner felt a little panic before the meeting and implored his deacon at Byerland, Howard Eshleman, to come.

As members of the committee fielded questions from Kendig, Ivan, Emanuel, Edwin, Howard, Martin, and Harvey, they did more than read the constitution to answer them; they secretly read the kind of men they had for the job at hand.

As Andrew Shaub led in a closing prayer, James Hess realized the die was about to be cast. He assumed, too, that soon this committee could again stop meeting and let another committee run the auto plan.

Mellinger Mennonite Church where the first Brotherly Aid Liability Plan operating committee was chosen in 1954

The first Brotherly Aid Liability Plan administrative committee (L-R): Kendig Miller, secretary; Edwin Gehman, chairman; Ivan Leaman, treasurer

Gehman, Leaman, Miller Chosen

Nine days later, September 13, 1954 at 4:30 p.m., the committee gathered at Mellingers again. This time even Peter Smith was present. Now the weight of the decision before the group started to bear on Stoner. He called on Peter "to lead in prayer seeking divine guidance" in the discernment at hand.

By votes, the committee chose Edwin Gehman as chair, J. Kendig Miller as secretary, and Ivan Leaman as treasurer. Elected as additional members were Emanual Martin of Annville, Earl Nissley of Middletown, Levi Smoker of Kinzers, and John Harnish of Washington Boro.

This operating group and the sponsoring committee had a joint meeting at Elmer Martin's house nine days later, Wednesday evening, September 22, 1954. As Simon Bucher led the closing prayer at Elmer Martin's house, Stoner must have felt the mantle of responsibility pass from his shoulder to the Gehman-Leaman-Miller team.

The Plan was up and running January 1, 1955. By January 17, 1955, they decided to investigate whether a charter by the Commonwealth was required and whether participants in the Liability Plan could enter the Mennonite Automobile Aid, Inc., plan for collision/comprehensive benefits.

Now the Brotherly Aid Sponsoring Committee had birthed its second offspring.

Committee Oversees Two Plans

A joint meeting at a central location, East Chestnut Street Mennonite Church in Lancaster, brought together the committee itself and its two offspring, the Fire and Storm Plan and the Liability Plan. Edwin Gehman reported that, by August 1, 355 people had signed 538 agreements, and already eight losses totaling $799.45 had been paid, leaving a balance of $4,065.95 in the coffers of the Liability Plan.

Roy Ulrich of the Fire and Storm Plan politely smiled in appreciation of those figures from the "younger brother." But the figures that he brought in his vest pocket to report for that year would make the Liability Plan look minuscule. In the current year, Roy noted, showing no emotion, losses alone were almost $31,000. Valuation by this time was $27 million. Besides, the Fire and Storm committee members were getting $1.38 per hour for their time. The Brotherly Aid Liability Plan people so far had received nothing.

At the Chestnut Street church the three distinct administrative groups (the sponsoring committee, the Fire and Storm Plan General Committee, and the Liability Plan General Committee) became acquainted for the first time. Before the meeting ended, the sponsoring committee of Brotherly Aid,

John and Ruth Harnish. John was elected to the first Brotherly Aid Liability Plan Committee in 1954. He wrote his first Brotherly Aid Liability Plan Agreement in 1955, and continued serving as BALP representative until he retired in 1995.

a Bishop Board appointed committee, made its first parental decisions for the two "boys"—that the two Plans share the same annual meeting and that they have fiscal years ending the same day.

The Brotherly Aid Liability Plan was born and on its own. Would its first steps prove to be as interesting to watch as the Fire and Storm Plan's had been?

— Chapter 8 —

The Cottage Years

Because the Fire and Storm Plan had been managed so well, the Liability Plan came into being with little problem. The Fire and Storm Plan had to face the theological questions, the institutional hurdles, and the popular fears against it.

Forty-five years after the fact, it is hard to recreate the resistance people felt against insurance. How did they define their opposition—or rather their conviction for spontaneous aid—in 1948? The basis for those convictions was the New Testament order of face-to-face resolving of conflicts in the church. However, insurance required lawsuits rather than mediation to settle many claims. The subrogation clause in most policies permitted an insurance company to sue in the policyholder's name. By signing a policy containing a subrogation clause, I might see my name in the newspaper as suing my deacon or sister over the slightest accident.

The "unequal yoke" (not becoming too involved with nonbelieving associates in business) was another conviction against insurance. How could I participate in an insurance company when my payment might help rebuild a bar or dance hall that burned down? Furthermore, God may want to use a physical loss to teach me a spiritual lesson. Does insurance limit God's will or make me forget consequences of wrong behavior?[39]

Why were people willing to consider liability insurance in 1955? Several reasons seem possible.

First, people rethought the functions of "insurance." They began to see a church plan as "a systematic way to care for one another." The old question, "Why don't we just trust God?" had little appeal when trust implied not taking precautions.

The "trust God" sentiment echoed the private side of religion, the individual contract between God and the believer. The "care" sentiment reached deeper into the Mennonite communal sense of life: "Am I my brother's keeper?" and "Give us this day our daily bread."

Second, the church was accepting of more organization and staff to manage it. The fear of church structure and written arrangements among neighbors and church members was real but less intense. People began to feel that the Spirit can prompt me to help the brother whose barn burned by paying a "bill."

Third, a precedent was already set. The conference already had a plan—Fire and Storm. What is the problem with adding to it auto liability, which

*By the 1950s, the automobile was captivating the American
consciousness with signs such as:
The Rambler and the Cadillac;
Christ is your engine, faith is your steering wheel;
Give me oil in my Ford, keep me truckin' for the Lord.*

the state seems to favor although not yet require? People's livelihoods depended less on tilling the soil and more on structures and machinery. After all, soil cannot burn. But, a plumber's truck can be totally wrecked.

When the Brotherly Aid Liability Plan formed, the church did not have to repeat the rationale for having a systematic plan. It had just settled that in 1950. Concern shifted to the lack of responsibility shown to the "neighbor" if liability were not covered. Not having liability was becoming a moral fault—and would eventually be contrary to the civil law.

Complexities of Automobile Law

The Brotherly Aid Liability Plan did not have to face the pre-WWII anti-insurance sentiments that the Fire and Storm Plan faced. However, it did have its own difficulties with the complexities of automobile ownership and the increasing expense associated with it. The livelihoods of an increasing number of Mennonites related to the car: fuel, repair, accessories, and sales, for example. In the United States, net auto insurance premiums written in 1948 and those written in 1953 show a jump from $2 billion to over $4 billion.[40]

The auto spawned its own bureaucracy of licensing and laws, not to mention the difficulty of litigation. If members of conference could handle one part of this and share as a caring Christian fellowship, could anyone object? No one would object seriously.

But one company, Goodville Mutual, would resist slightly. Goodville thought of itself as a Mennonite organization. Informally it was. But it was a company that consisted mostly of people who were Mennonite. The church exercised no official oversight, although Goodville was a founding member of the Association of Mennonite Aid Societies.

Independent mutual companies, even when called Mennonite, had developed constitutions that could not be altered easily. In order to be related and subject to the church, new plans had to form. Modifying existing structure was practically a legal impossibility.

The year 1955 came and a new name entered the church vocabulary: Brotherly Aid Liability Plan.

This new Brotherly Aid Liability Plan committee was just one among many other new initiatives on the church agenda: Philhaven Hospital; Lancaster Mennonite School; Locust Grove, Kraybill, and other elementary schools; Mennonite Mutual Aid; camps; an historical library; retirement institutions; and many new congregations.

Meanwhile, the property Plan, Fire and Storm, quietly grew and faced matters one at a time with practically no fear of litigation. The Brotherly Aid Liability Plan instantly faced state laws, local highway laws, and claims from persons who were not necessarily Christian, let alone Mennonite.

While Clarence Harnish of Fire and Storm rarely brought any matters to the Brotherly Aid Sponsoring Committee, the Brotherly Aid Liability Plan from its inception relied on that committee for advice. In fact, after the Brotherly Aid Liability Plan was up and running on January 1, 1955, its General Committee (Miller, Leaman, and Gehman) met jointly with the Brotherly Aid committee at least twice in 1955 and again early in 1956 to hammer out technical problems such as:

• Whether the Brotherly Aid Plans should be registered with the state. (Decided to leave Fire and Storm without a Pennsylvania charter, but appointed a committee of the Brotherly Aid Liability Plan General Committee plus Krady, Smith, and Hess to "investigate the need of registry or obtaining a charter in Pennsylvania" for the Brotherly Aid Liability Plan.)

• Whether to allow Brotherly Aid Liability Plan members to use Mennonite Auto Aid for collision. (Deferred until later.)

• Whether to have an annual assessment. (Sentiment against building up a large bank balance; "possibly an annual offering for relief.")

• Whether to accept members from Franconia Conference. (August 8, 1955, voted yes.)

- Whether to accept Ohio Conference members. (Yes.)

- Whether to accept tractor trailers. (No.)

- Whether to cover a plumber whose contract requires each truck to be covered by a $100,000 policy. ("What can you do for me?" Answer: "Nothing.")

- Whether the Brotherly Aid Liability Plan can give some money to pay funeral expenses to a participant involved in an accident in which a child was killed. The participant was absolved of all blame but wants to bear that cost as a Christian duty. (Let him do it personally; constitution does not permit such payments.)

- Whether to open the Plans to other church groups. ("Agreed that we continue to permit both Brotherly Aid plans to accept others of like faith and standing into the plans at their discretion with the counsel of the standing committee.")

Other Early Brotherly Aid Liability Plan Issues

The first Bishop Board meeting after the Brotherly Aid Liability Plan was in operation was held January 21, 1955 at East Petersburg. From the start, the Brotherly Aid Sponsoring Committee kept the bishops apprised of the developments in the Liability Plan. The complexities of auto liability stamped Brotherly Aid Liability Plan from its birth as a gregarious, collaborating church program. A farm in Manheim never moved to Mascot. However, a car in Virginia today might be in Illinois tomorrow.

Right before the bishops adjourned that Friday in early 1955, Elmer and Stoner, with Simon helping them on the technical details, reported that they were studying whether the Brotherly Aid Liability Plan needs a state charter. In September 1955 the Brotherly Aid Committee reported that the Brotherly Aid Liability Plan does not need certification with the state.

A few months later, in February 1956, another bishop entered the conversation—J. Paul Graybill. Now that he was out of the principal's harness at Lancaster Mennonite School, he turned his thoughts to new matters. What should we recommend regarding hospitalization insurance? he asked his fellow bishops. The Bishop Board minutes recorded the answer: "Since hospital insurance is generally left optional, it was agreed to refer this matter to the local church leaders."

At the same meeting in 1956, J. Paul introduced John Burkholder, who represented Mennonite Auto Aid collision in Virginia. John, seeing Stoner

Bishop J. Paul Graybill
asked the Bishop Board in 1957 to take a position on hospitalization.

and Elmer in the circle of elders, "made clear that Mennonite Auto Aid is not liability," the minutes of the bishops noted.

While the bishops rarely had Fire and Storm Plan items on the agenda since it started in 1950, the Brotherly Aid Liability Plan kept appearing in Bishop Board minutes after 1955. Edwin Gehman saw as early as May 1956 that Lancaster and Franconia as conferences needed a policy regarding Franconia's participation in the Plan, rather than deciding each case individually.

The Brotherly Aid Liability Plan's Home in Leola

Once the Brotherly Aid Liability Plan general committee was appointed in October 1954, it began to meet with a clock-like, railroad regularity—every two weeks—at the home of J. Kendig and Anna Miller in central Leola, 1 Mayfield Drive, along Route 23, across from the 1949 War Memorial building. The Miller's brick, two-story house had been built in 1938. The Miller's purchased it in 1943 for $8,000.[41]

These men in mid-life (Kendig, 41; Ivan, 48; and Edwin, 53) threw themselves with conviction into doing everything it took to begin an auto liability plan. Kendig's career with PP&L was already midway in 1954.

The Brotherly Aid Liability Plan office from 1955-1959 was in the home of J. Kendig Miller, Leola, Pennsylvania. The first BALP committee met at Kendig's home 140 times during these five years.

He worked for the electric company from 1932 to 1978. Ivan was firmly established at the Ezra Martin meat company. Kendig recalls that at 6:30 or 7:00 p.m. they would gather and meet as late as 10:00 p.m. if the business required it, even though Ivan would say that "you can't make a good decision after 8:00."

Although Earl Nissley and John Harnish met with them the first time (October 21, 1954), by the next week (October 28) the trio of Kendig, Ivan, and Edwin was established as the working group. After that Nissley and Harnish did not regularly come to the working sessions.

Within the first year (until October 20, 1955), this dedicated trio attended their 27 regular meetings and six special meetings—two regular meetings with the Brotherly Aid committee, one with the Brotherly Aid committee to plan the annual meeting, and three to consider special cases and general policies.[42]

Their work was monumental. Treasurer Ivan, for example, in that first year, in his meticulous longhand, wrote 620 entries in the ledgers. Each consisted of full name, address (no ZIP code yet), and information that required about 12 other digits. When Earl W. Rohrer and Landis E. Hershey audited the books at the end of the first year they "found his work to be very neat and accurate," they wrote.

But if Ivan thought he had found his stride that first year, the avalanche had hardly begun. In his second year of Brotherly Aid Liability Plan bookkeeping, Ivan tallied up almost twice as many entries—1,185. All were neatly entered in fountain pen. Erasures were rare.

Meanwhile, Edwin Gehman, chair of the Brotherly Aid Liability Plan trio, was troubleshooting, responding to local committee questions, investigating accidents. One trip took him as far as Ohio. The secretary, Kendig, had enclosed a portion of his porch to serve as the office, equipped with a file cabinet, a desk, a portable typewriter, and a card file. During the fifth year of Brotherly Aid Liability Plan work, Kendig tallied 500 hours; his wife, Anna, 80 hours. In full-time equivalency that was for Kendig and Anna together 11 and one-half hours a week—almost one and a half days per week.

First Local Liability Committees Appointed

Not only did the Brotherly Aid Liability Plan trio do the work described above, they also initiated local committees. The first local committee was from Millwood, then Cottage City, Maryland, then Hanover, Pennsylvania. The earliest interest came from some distance from the geographic center of Lancaster Conference.

Even though in October 1954 the Fire and Storm Plan had a balance of $13,797, Ivan personally loaned $300 to the Brotherly Aid Liability Plan to open the bank account. It never occurred to him to borrow from the elder

First office equipment
of the Brotherly Aid Liability Plan

Plan. From the beginning, the two Plans followed separate administrative paths, while sharing the concept. Three months later the Brotherly Aid Liability Plan had generated enough registration fees for Ivan to have his money returned (at no interest). A year and a half later (May 1, 1956), Edwin loaned $2,500 to the plan—this time at three percent interest—to pay a claim of nearly $4,000 to Amos Z. Longenecker of Elizabethtown. When the Plan began, members submitted claims to pay what they could not afford. In most cases, members paid claims against their own situations as though self-insured, and later sought reimbursement from the Plan. In later years, when settling claims became much more complicated and the legal climate had changed, the job of settling claims became part of the administrative committee's role and claims were paid on behalf of the members.

The Brotherly Aid Liability Plan went into operation January 1, 1955, and by the January 31 meeting the committee had to pay the first claim—$114.31 to Richard Garman of Route 2, Mount Joy, Pennsylvania. By March, the trio processed the first cancellation—Charlotte McCorkel canceled because of a growing conviction that she was trusting in the "arm of flesh rather than God."

By April, the trio would have read an *Intelligencer Journal* editorial, "Financially Irresponsible Motorist," and felt satisfied that they were offering a low-cost way for Mennonites to avoid irresponsible driving. The editorial lambasted car owners without insurance.[43]

In June 1955, a Marlin Weaver claim in Virginia brought headaches. The need for posting a bond and providing papers for members to carry when on long auto trips became clear. In that same month a Brotherly Aid Liability Plan member from McAlisterville hit and killed a young boy who had darted onto the roadway from behind a parked car. Later that summer a teenage member of the Plan, James Lapp, the son of John E. who had spoken at

Over the years, the number of Brotherly Aid Liability Plan members included some who have served the church widely. James M. Lapp, General Secretary of the Mennonite Church from September 1987 to November 1995, incurred one of the first accidents covered by the Brotherly Aid Liability Plan. BALP paid out $326.72 for his accident. Jim's next assessment continued at a mere $10.00.

Byerland in 1948, bought a 1954 Chevy. He enrolled it as agreement number 909 and paid the $10 initial fee. One Saturday afternoon, eager to go hunting, James drove out of his father's driveway onto the Allentown Pike without looking. He entered the path of a man, he recalls, of African-American ancestry driving an early 1950s Ford. Nobody was hurt.[44]

Yet the police charged the driver of the Ford for not blowing his horn. In later years James related that "this could be racism that I didn't recognize at that time." The Brotherly Aid Liability Plan paid out $326.72 for teenager Lapp's irresponsibility. Yet, the correlation between young drivers and the number of accidents did not go unnoticed. Four years later age scales were instituted.

Already in the first year of operation, I-W boys in alternate service to the military draft were applying from distant areas. People preparing to take long car trips asked for special papers valid in all states. A Conservative Conference congregation in Florida asked to join the Plan. Elton Moshier, a teacher at Lancaster Mennonite School, requested 26 copies of the Brotherly Aid Liability Plan constitution for class use. "I always thought students should be aware of the economic aspects of their faith," he told the writer.[45]

The trio fielded requests from Greenwood, Delaware, and Brutus, Kentucky. They explained the Plan at Chambersburg, Belleville, Franconia, and Harrisonburg, Virginia. One member transferred to the new Monterey congregation (Ohio and Eastern Conference) and had to cancel. (This resistance to the Ohio and Eastern Conference soon changed.) A teenager in a Philadelphia congregation joined the Air Force and forfeited his participation. Changes in New York state law ruled out Brotherly Aid Liability Plan coverage there.

If this weren't enough for the fledgling trio to handle in one year, one of the insurance men who had met at Stoner Krady's in 1949 before the founding of the first plan, now, at the end of Brotherly Aid Liability Plan's first year of operation badgered Stoner Krady again: How can Stoner justify operating the Brotherly Aid Liability Plan "without the counsel of the church"?[46]

Stoner must have been getting thick skin by now because he had plenty of other gripes against him in these years after 1955—an aborted deacon ordination at East Chestnut Street, various difficulties in some other Lancaster congregations, and difficulties in holding people to the Rules and Discipline.

Workload Increases

Before the end of the first hectic year, the workload was already a concern. By the end of the summer of 1955, the Brotherly Aid Liability Plan trio met with the Brotherly Aid Sponsoring Committee at Ivan's house along the Old Philadelphia Pike. Together they looked at the workload that loomed ahead of them as the Plan kept growing.

By the end of 1956, Edwin, Ivan, and Kendig received payments of $300, $350, and $450, respectively, for their labor. One year later Kendig's reimbursement rose to $500. Yet the ardor of the original trio did not abate. Every other Monday without fail they gathered in Leola and did the staff work of the Brotherly Aid Liability Plan. Compared to the leisurely pace of the Fire and Storm Plan, which had only 61 losses in 1958, the Brotherly Aid Liability Plan had all the nervous energy of a busy highway intersection: 113 claims paid that year, each one taking more time to resolve than the property claims, each one closer to the treacherous waters of litigation.

Yet the system held. Handling claims, taking policy issues to the Sponsoring Committee, processing local committees, keeping abreast of state law, auditing the books, planning annual meetings, writing assessments, holding public meetings—a dizzying whirlwind of paper activity on the front porch of the brick house in Leola, every other Monday evening.

With their regular full-time work Kendig and Anna sometimes wondered how long it could last. Ivan and Ethel and their eight children, the youngest turning ten, could feel the pressure. Edwin and his wife seemed to thrive on the extra work.

By late December 1957, some help in the treasurer's role for Ivan seemed to be needed. The trio felt a search should begin, but it was nine months later before an assistant was appointed.

A lot can happen in nine months.

The Brotherly Aid Plan

For the Lancaster Mennonite Conference District

CLARENCE H. HARNISH, *Chairman*

The interest in the *Brotherly Aid Plan* has finally crystallized. The plan is now available whereby the brethren of the Lancaster Mennonite Conference area may systematically help bear one another's burden in relation to loss by fire, storm, or lightning, of building and contents.

This organization has been effected by permission of and subject to the executive board of Lancaster Conference. It consists of a chairman, a secretary, and a treasurer. There are also local committees in each area as the need arises.

Brethren wishing to participate in this plan may write to Clarence H. Harnish, Chairman of General Committee, Lancaster, R. 7, Pa., or inquire from their local committee members. Copies of the printed constitution will gladly be sent on request.

Roy Ulrich, Lancaster, R. 4, Pa., is secretary, and Andrew Shaub, Lancaster, R. 1, Pa., is treasurer of the general committee.

---

*Copy of first Brotherly Aid Liability Plan agreement
written for Edwin Gehman's 1948 Plymouth*

— Chapter 9 —

Some Founders Retire

The trio that had met for 100 consecutive biweekly meetings, each ending with the Lord's Prayer, implored the Brotherly Aid Sponsoring Committee for help. The deeply committed but over-extended chair, secretary, and treasurer of the Liability Plan urgently presented workload problems. Kendig told the sponsoring committee, for example, that in 1958 his work for the Brotherly Aid Liability Plan had increased 40 percent over 1957.

Kendig would already have reached the breaking point if his wife, Anna, hadn't been willing to come to the rescue and help him, working at least one hour for every six he did. The electric company was demanding more time from Kendig and was expecting him to respond to service calls even in the middle of the night.[47]

Even though the secretary's plea was sincere and probably the most urgent, the sponsoring committee chose to first fix the treasurer's workload. After all, Ivan had been ordained a minister in 1955. The board considered several persons as potential assistant treasurers and by October 6 engaged David Buckwalter, who began to come to the meetings. Ivan remained treasurer but stopped coming to the biweekly staff meetings.

The sponsoring committee needed more time to decide on help for the secretary, who had the heaviest load. His home was the home of the Brotherly Aid Liability Plan. Changing the secretary and hence the address of the Plan too hastily might send a signal of instability.

Fire and Storm Work Increases

The Fire and Storm Plan, of course, also did its office work in the homes of its operating committee members. Although the regular meetings rotated among the three, when it was time to prepare the mailing for the annual meeting, Clarence, Roy, and Andrew got together at Clarence's house. He had more room to prepare and stuff envelopes for mailing the annual statements. "We folded and folded and folded," Andrew recalled years later. Clarence's sisters would sing a few songs for them. No radio or record player provided background sound.

Andrew, as early as 1955, with four young children at home, had sent a letter to the Bishop Board requesting not to serve on any committees. As a result Howard Witmer took his place on the Itinerant Evangelism Com-mittee and Carl Keener replaced him on the Peace Committee.

Andrew kept his work as deacon at Rohrerstown and his place on the Brotherly Aid Sponsoring Committee. But after ten years of service on this committee and on the Fire and Storm general committee, he reconsidered. In 1958, because of the pressure, he wrote a letter to James H. Hess, secretary of the sponsoring committee, tendering his resignation as treasurer of the Fire and Storm Plan.[48] At almost the same time James received a letter of resignation from Kendig.

Key players of both plans wanted out. James called Stoner at Krady Hollow and gave him the bad news. The two decided to call a special meeting of the Brotherly Aid Sponsoring Committee at the Mellinger meetinghouse for the evening of September 14, 1958.

After James' call, Stoner himself, who served this cause since 1948, said something to Frances about moving on if the times were changing. "Could a bishop resign?" he must have wondered. His heart was following Jewish evangelism for the past nine years, and the mission board had just asked him to move to Philadelphia and lead the Messianic Fellowship Center there. He had already been mulling over this when he heard of Kendig's and Andrew's resignations. Personal evangelism had always been his first love. He hadn't known happier work than his days as superintendent of Vine Street mission. The call to similar work in Philadelphia seemed irresistible.

When the old team somberly met, the word of Kendig's and Andrew's resignation letters had already leaked to Martin, Hess, Bucher, and the rest. So many changes since 1948!

To spread the work on more shoulders, the group decided to "consider" dividing both of the Brotherly Aid plans into districts, James wrote in the minutes. Afraid that Stoner was moving this too fast, James bargained for time by using the word "consider." He had seen Stoner quietly divesting himself of church work the last couple of years, with Frank Enck tapped for oversight of the Lancaster congregations and more recently James' young brother-in-law, David Thomas, for the New Danville ones.

After the discussion of reorganizing the plans, Stoner moved the discussion to Kendig's resignation letter. Replacements were suggested: Raymond Sauder, Earl Rohrer, Clarence Rohrer, Lloyd Nissley, Willis Detweiler, Luke Mosemann, John Kennel, John Harnish, and Robert Gochnauer.

Before the committee adjourned, and after agreeing to meet again at 7:00 p.m. September 25 at LMS, they gave Stoner what no one knew would be his final assignment for Brotherly Aid: take these names to the Bishop Board and ask for further counsel regarding a person to replace Kendig.

Stoner Krady Resigns

It was a hectic week for Stoner. Jewish evangelism under the mission board offered him a chance to grow and leave the wearisome administrative duties of the Bishop Board behind, to say nothing of leaving the vegetables and goats of Krady Hollow for a steady check. A year ago he had told the Bishop Board of his interest in Jewish evangelism. That is when he got permission to ordain Frank Enck for the Lancaster district.

When Stoner went to the September 1958 Bishop Board, the biggest resignation he had to drop in their laps was not Kendig's or Andrew's, but his own—from the Brotherly Aid Sponsoring Committee and from the Lancaster-New Danville district.

He told all of this to his fellow bishops with some emotion. He looked over at Elmer for support. They both would soon turn 65 years old, a good time to change duties. Elmer would understand if he resigned, although Elmer would not quit himself. James Hess would continue the good fight, he knew.

Stoner Krady laid down his mantle and his laurels as the founding chair of the sponsoring committee. As an agenda item that day, his resignation immediately followed a report about interest in a ramshackle building close to New Danville. Called the Herr House, it was built in 1719. It was in such bad repair and abandonment that the Fire and Storm Plan would probably not cover it if asked.

Although Stoner resigned from Brotherly Aid, his stature cast a long shadow that would still help define mutual aid in the churches around Lancaster for many years to come. He had brought the people a long way. He had seen the promised land. But he resigned a few months too early to take the name of Kendig's successor, John Shenk, to the Bishop Board. John would lead in Brotherly Aid endeavors for two generations. John's name would become synonymous with Brotherly Aid.

Clair and Verna Eby. In 1958, Clair Eby succeeded founder Stoner Krady on the Brotherly Aid Sponsoring Committee.

When the Brotherly Aid sponsoring committee met at Lancaster Mennonite School on September 25, 1958, it elected Bucher to Stoner's empty chair. It then welcomed a brand new bishop, Clair Eby, a respectable 45 years old, whom the Bishop Board elected to replace Stoner.

Brotherly Aid's first decade was drawing to a close. And again there were personnel to find.

John Shenk, James H. Hess, and J. Kendig Miller reunite in 1994 on the porch where years earlier, John had been asked to join the Brotherly Aid team.

— *Chapter 10* —

John B. Shenk Joins Liability Team

The Dade County Accident

It started simply enough in Dade County, Florida in the Redland Labor Camp in the town of Homestead in a Voluntary Service unit. One Saturday evening Miriam Dick asked Daniel Shertzer if she could borrow his car to drive into town. It was her first time driving in Homestead.

At 8:30 p.m., Miriam didn't see a stop sign at the corner of 8th Street and G Avenue Northwest and a '53 Chevrolet hit Daniel's car. The '53 Chevy cost about $200 to fix and the four people were treated in the hospital. Three of them were released, but one "might possibly have internal injuries," Daniel wrote immediately to Kendig.

That was in 1957, two years after the Brotherly Aid Liability Plan began. Daniel went into action almost immediately, contacting the people. As he got overwhelmed, another Volunteer Service worker in the unit, John Shenk, offered to help. The collision caused the injured woman to miss two months of work. One of her cousins was a lawyer.

When John learned that complications could ensue, he engaged the service of a lawyer, contacted the Florida claims office in Miami, and reported to the Brotherly Aid Liability Plan committee. A 700-word letter to Kendig in February 1957 ended with these words: "Before closing I would like to say that I am finding this experience quite rewarding, even though it is a bit frustrating sometimes. I am looking forward to an opportunity to further discuss the philosophy of Brotherly Aid with you or other members of the committee when I return to the county. Yours in the service of Christ."

Shenks Return to Brenneman Homestead

The "return to the county" came in the spring of 1959.

After two happy years of Voluntary Service in Florida, John and Myrtle Brenneman Shenk resisted the thought of leaving the work with the seasonal agricultural workers and their children. The second year John had become the unit leader of the Homestead Voluntary Service group. Their term of service officially ended in the fall. With nothing else beckoning, they considered staying longer. They weighed their options and finally told Paul Landis, Voluntary Service administrator, to count on them to stay through the winter. Paul was pleased but surprised. He thought that John might feel overqualified for routine Voluntary Service work.[49]

When spring came to Florida, the children of migrant workers went off to farm work in other states, John and Myrtle loaded up Leroy Mellinger's Olds 88 and a borrowed homemade trailer with the few belongings they owned, fired up the mighty V8 engine, and headed north on U.S. 1.

The future looked bright but unknown as they entered Georgia. Suddenly, a terrific racket jolted them out of their pleasant ride. Pulling the Olds onto the berm, John expected the worst. Fortunately, it was only a loose fender skirt dragging on the road. Snapping it back into place, John thought that cars can both take you to a future and confuse the present.

The Olds got them safely to the farm of Myrtle's parents south of Millersville, where they took up temporary residence. John worked weekdays on Earl King's carpenter crew.[50]

The Brennemans were good hosts to the young couple trying to get their feet on the ground. On humid summer evenings they had the farmhouse porch all to themselves to dream the dreams of newlyweds.

Kendig Tries to Resign

The times that Kendig and Anna Miller could sit on their porch were fewer and fewer. Instead of offering them a safe haven from the pressures of life, their porch in Leola reminded them of claims to process, minutes to type, and letters to write. Kendig's resignation letter, now one year old, was still waiting for action. Kendig had no second thoughts about the letter of resignation he had sent to James Hess.

Yes, he was glad to have his name on the Liability Plan document that stated: "I agree to share...in the burden of any liability for bodily injury and/or property damage that God may see fit to allow to come into the experience of any one of us." But he and Anna had joyfully served five years on marginal time.

That plea to find a successor had been in the sponsoring committee's hands since fall 1958. For some reason finding his successor was moving at a very slow—or providential—pace.

But it was moving. Although the Brotherly Aid Liability Plan got most of the parent committee's attention, the Brotherly Aid committee first attended to the needs of the elder Plan, which by then was covering property valued at more than $41 million. "If Bro. Earl Rohrer is not used in the Fire and Storm Plan, he shall be asked to serve as secretary of the Liability Plan," the committee decided.

But Earl, a 1945 Lancaster Mennonite School graduate (and an accounting whiz under the tutelage of Clyde Stoner), was fully immersed in his father's seed business with no time to spare.

By January 24, 1959, no successor for Kendig was yet in sight. On that Saturday afternoon at Lancaster Mennonite School, the Brotherly Aid Fire and Storm Plan, the Brotherly Aid Liability Plan, and the Brotherly Aid Sponsoring Committee met. Raymond Sauder was introduced as the new treasurer to take Andrew Shaub's place on the Fire and Storm general committee. Andrew would remain on the Sponsoring Committee. Then James Hess read again the stale news in the letter from Kendig. Who could replace him?

John Fisher, the son of the deacon at Rossmere, and Earl Zimmerman were suggested. Kendig did not know either of these men very well, but he was certain he and Anna and son Glenn could soon have their porch back and focus entirely on his PP&L work. Winter slowly turned into spring.

When John Fisher and Earl Zimmerman did not materialize as replacements, Kendig recalled John Shenk, the young VSer who had negotiated with the Miami attorney who wanted $37,500 for the claim. John, by a patient explanation of the Christian philosophy of the Plan, held the final cost down to $5,306. Kendig could think of no one who could handle his work better. And John was coming back to the Lancaster area in just days.

The John and Myrtle Shenk home (house to the right) near Lititz where Brotherly Aid had its office from 1960-1965

Weaver Bookstore about 1959 where special strategy meetings were held during Stoner Krady's days of working here. John Shenk also worked at the bookstore in the 1960s.

So on May 28, 1959, John's name appeared at the top of the list that the Brotherly Aid Sponsoring Committee prepared, followed by Norman Glick, Stanley Kreider, and Ray Yost.

These three would never hear about their desirability to the Brotherly Aid Liability Plan, because the first prospect materialized.

One evening James Hess and Kendig, driving his 1956 Dodge, found John and Myrtle on the porch of the Brenneman home. They asked him to assist Kendig. John and Myrtle had one child but no church responsibilities at the time. John recalled the thrilling moments in Miami responding to the Watkins' attorney's inflated claim of $37,500. He remembered being captivated by the philosophy of Brotherly Aid in the hot, dry Dade County sun; he could think of no better prospect in the offing for a college graduate with one-half seminary degree. John said yes. He had no idea that Kendig had sent his letter of resignation to the committee over a full year earlier.

On July 13, 1959, John made his first of many trips east on Route 23 to Leola, where his letters and telephone calls had gone during the Watkins tribulation.

Shenk Succeeds Miller

Seeing John's aptitude, Kendig invited him to take over the work of secretary. John accepted. John took his first minutes as secretary on Kendig's enclosed porch office on January 11, 1960. The next week the Brotherly Aid Liability Plan office, with a balance of $36,695 on the books, moved up the Newport Road to Lititz. On January 25 the Brotherly Aid Liability Plan committee of Gehman, Buckwalter (filling in for Ivan Leaman), and Shenk met at Lititz, where the office would reside for the next 103 meetings, until April 5, 1965.

In those five and a quarter years, John and Myrtle threw themselves into the Brotherly Aid Liability Plan with youthful vigor and vision. He was 29 years old in January 1960; immediately he saw room for improvements.

First, due to his scant income, he asked for an advance. As Kendig and Anna were bowing out they together received $700, which in 1959 represented about two months pay to a church worker. Lancaster Mennonite School teachers that year received about $300 per teaching month. For example, Elton Moshier, who used the Brotherly Aid constitution in his classes, received exactly $297.77 in September 1959 for teaching there. (Salaries varied by family need.) So $700 was two and a third months of Lancaster Mennonite School-rate labor.[51]

Rather than waiting 12 months to get paid, John requested payment by the quarter. The other officers of the Plan were glad to do that too. John's humble fearlessness to face the powers of state and court immediately proved useful. Several Brotherly Aid Liability Plan members did not receive their due reimbursement, and he went to Harrisburg to put pressure on the system and got results.

An Isaac and Naomi Beiler case loomed as high as $20,000. The Liability Plan General Committee called a special meeting in the back of Weaver Book Store in Lancaster in April 1960 to plan strategy. John had learned about the legal game in Florida and could challenge the aggressiveness of lawyers. His experience out of state proved useful by May when a Leroy Smoker claim in Arizona required that a security deposit be posted in Arizona.

Devotion to the local church program never lapsed. In July the Brotherly Aid Liability Plan General Committee moved its "sacred" Monday evening meeting to Thursday so as not to interfere with summer Bible school. Hammer Creek and several other churches had a bus to gather children, and the Brotherly Aid Liability Plan accepted the bus into the Plan, lowering the assessment to reflect the limited time the bus was in use.

Shenk Institutes New Procedures

In his first years, operating the Brotherly Aid Liability Plan out of his kitchen, John established his style of moving cautiously ahead. He renamed the general committee, which was the operating group of the Plan, the administrative committee. Semimonthly meetings became monthly, as fewer routine operations needed to come to the attention of the whole committee. He modified the minutes. He urged that members of the Plan have a voice on issues. He established an open line of credit with Lancaster County National Bank. He took unique issues to the Brotherly Aid Sponsoring Committee. He revised the constitution. To further streamline the routine he became the assistant treasurer when David Buckwalter resigned from that post so he could write checks between meetings.

John also increased communication with the local committees. An attempt was made in the Belleville area to empower the local committee to do more of the work. He brought to the annual meeting a motion to raise assessments for certain groups of members based on risk (primarily young and unmarried operators) and it passed. However in 1964 his motion to begin a $35 deductible did not pass. He also began to fine-tune the reports on the types of claims involving persons of various ages. In 1962 the 161 Brotherly Aid Liability Plan claims averaged $151.40 each.

In 1963, his third year with the Brotherly Aid Liability Plan and at the age of 33, John was ordained to the ministry at East Petersburg Mennonite Church, at that time a non-salary position. Now he had three assignments: working in the Provident Bookstore (which followed his construction job), secretary for the Brotherly Aid Liability Plan, and minister at East Petersburg Mennonite Church.

Other Groups Join Liability Plan

By 1963, the Brotherly Aid Liability Plan reports noted that Brotherly Aid Liability Plan participants were associated with these church bodies:

Lancaster Conference	57.6%
Franconia Conference	14.3
Beachy Amish	8.5
Old Order Mennonite	7.5
Conservative Conference	3.2
Allegheny Conference	2.7
Ohio Conference	2.5
Franklin Conference	1.5
Other groups	2.2

Howard Raid at the Mutual Aid Archives Library, Bluffton, Ohio. Howard was an enthusiastic promoter of mutual aid and had a positive influence on John Shenk.

The Brotherly Aid Liability Plan became attractive to other groups, and because others joined by 1964 the percentage of Lancaster Mennonite Conference participants fell to 54.7 percent. By 1977, it was 43 percent. In 1981, Lancaster Mennonite Conference was approaching 39 percent, while Franconia had steadily risen to 24 percent. The 1964 report also noted that 28.5 percent of members were ages 16-25, an age category for which most insurance companies set high fees. The Brotherly Aid Liability Plan had quite a future if it held on to its youngest members, John could see.

Two years after Kendig resigned and John Shenk returned from Florida, the chair, Edwin Gehman, who was ordained in 1961, reported that he would be moving to be a minister in the Tamaqua, Pennsylvania mission.

Changes on Other Fronts

When the sponsoring committee gave the go-ahead to appoint John Shenk in 1959, someone on the committee suggested creating a full-time position, but the committee thought this would jeopardize its status with the state. In 1959, Howard Raid of the Association of Mennonite Aid Societies, asked for permission to visit Brotherly Aid along with other Mennonite Aid plans. The sponsoring committee "agreed to accept the visit" and share information, but "we have no interest in becoming part of the association."

The Brotherly Aid Sponsoring Committee and Brotherly Aid Liability Plan General Committee met just two months after John joined the team and approved a list of three attorneys: Young of Manheim, Carl Herr, and Ralph Eby. The committee also decided to "give such information to Mennonite Mutual Aid in cases where their and our participants were involved as will be of value to them."

Insurance issues were converging from several fronts. When the Brotherly Aid Sponsoring Committee reached out a hand to Mennonite Mutual Aid it had followed conference precedence.

If the Liability Plan for autos was modestly growing by one-third in John's kitchen from 2,030 vehicles in 1960 to 2,721 in 1965, another kind of burden was stirring impatiently in the wings, threatening to take center stage.

— *Chapter 11* —

Hospital Bills and Burdens To Share

As Americans used automobiles for more and more of their transportation, entertainment, socializing, and vacationing; as the layout of the suburbs required the use of autos for practically every errand and job; and as America built more streets and roads to accommodate these cars, the number of collisions per year rose.

The new roads were larger, straighter, and faster. And the collisions were more deadly. Highway fatalities in the United States in 1955 (the year the Brotherly Aid Liability Plan began) numbered 38,426. The number would keep climbing to 56,278 by 1972.[52]

Along with the highways grew up a new rescue and treatment industry to respond to the toll that speed, metal, glass, and fire wreaked on the macadam and ribbon concrete highways. Insurance costs grew to pay for the disasters on wheels. A new generation of ambulances, medical techniques, rescue equipment and new professions grew up alongside the favorite mode of travel. More Mennonites entered those professions, sometimes with a little guilt over the use of litigation and attorneys for settling disputes.

And the price of everything rose. While the Homestead claim of 1956 (that gave John Shenk his first field work) rattled the coffers of the Brotherly Aid Liability Plan, by 1960 $15,000 claims were routine.

With the increased human carnage of the 1960s, the increased size and power of cars, came a movement to make the highway safer. In 1965 Ralph Nader wrote *Unsafe at Any Speed*, an exposé of General Motor's Corvair and its fire danger in case of an accident. Seat belts for safety came to public consciousness slowly in the 1960s. The "sport" of driving and drinking came to arouse indignation in the average American driver. Magazines featuring cars appeared. State legislatures kept pressure on drivers who did not have liability insurance.

Auto Costs Increase

All of this spelled higher claims. In 1965 the average cost per Brotherly Aid Liability Plan claim was $382.62. In 1966 the plan had to borrow for a $39,000 loss, the "biggest in history of plan." If that amount sobered the driving in 1966, by 1971 one accident claim reached the stratospheric $100,000 figure, which required the Plan, for only the second time in its 16 years, to request an additional assessment.

By 1960, all medical costs were rising. Collisions on the highway as well as medical services for prolonged illness were changing people's idea of the medical industry. While the hometown physician who charged $3 a visit and sold pills from his office for another $4 dominated the medical landscape, now specialists were coming into their own, even specialized hospitals. By 1960, the family doctor may have charged you $10 to decide which specialist you needed to see.

Deacons in Lancaster Conference congregations saw old people lose their entire savings in one extended illness and were ready for the church to respond. While life insurance used to be the focus of health discussion, now it was eclipsed by new agenda: hospitalization.

Mennonite Mutual Aid Hospitalization Available

The Mennonite denomination's Mennonite Mutual Aid board had a hospitalization plan in place. MMA trained its eyes on the large Mennonite market in eastern Pennsylvania. The strategy to reach this market was to continue asking the question at the conference level and to quietly keep signing up participants on an individual basis.

Lancaster Conference did have a stake in the industry. After all, by 1952 the conference had its own mental hospital, Philhaven. Most bills for Philhaven's services were paid by the patient, the "first party," not by a "third party." Making a bogeyman of life insurance was becoming dated.

The employers where Mennonite people worked saw the need for hospital insurance and began offering it as a package along with the wages. Often the hospital package included a small life insurance policy. Earl B. Groff, the vice president of the mission board, worked for Eastern States (a farm supply business). He convinced Eastern States to make the life insurance part of the employment package optional. He reported the change to the Bishop Board as a very positive sign. Mennonites could join the modern world of employment yet hold to their prohibition on life insurance.

Bishop Board Allows Mennonite Mutual Aid for Individuals

At the May 1957 Bishop Board meeting, at East Petersburg Mennonite Church, the bishops finally held a "considerable discussion about Mennonite Mutual Aid...which phases of its work might be left optional to our members... which may be objectionable." Bishop Mahlon Zimmerman reported that a "brother in his district" who "lost his membership through life insurance" may be restored to the church by keeping the policy but deleting the death benefit. That issue was left to the local church.

By the next meeting, in June 1957, the Bishop Board concluded the Mennonite Mutual Aid issue by agreeing to "let Mennonite Mutual Aid services [be] optional to [the] individual." One year later they discussed the implications of Social Security. Again the bishops decided that "we leave persons act according to their consciences." Mutual aid appeared to be pushed off the conference agenda, leaving it up to the individual. To some that was a contradiction of "mutual" terms. But to others a welcome, liberalizing move.

The June Bishop Board decision was the opening Mennonite Mutual Aid wanted in Lancaster Conference. Yet MMA moved cautiously. Not until early 1962 did Mennonite Mutual Aid's director H. Ralph Hernley take a bold initiative by asking the Bishop Board to promote Mennonite Mutual Aid at the coming spring conference. But conference decided not to "promote at present Mennonite Mutual Aid in conference session."

Mennonite Mutual Aid was not getting very far very fast in the conference. But in their very own house the bishops saw one of their very own committees begin to move: the little-known Industrial Relations Committee. Formed originally to negotiate the treacherous labor union issues and feelings, it now recommended that a study be made of "the need of providing a health, hospitalization, burial, and survivors aid plan." The recommendation passed March 1962. The committee consisted of John S. Martin, Edwin H. Gehman, Ivan D. Leaman, and Andrew H. Shaub.

Conference Considers Hospitalization

By 1958, the people of Lancaster Mennonite Conference had formed their own historical society, youth paper, psychiatric care hospital, retirement home, and a number of elementary schools. There was also discussion about establishing a farm for missionary children. New mission fields were opening. The church horizons seemed unlimited.

Paul N. Kraybill, an executive at the mission board, proposed building a Lancaster Mennonite Conference general hospital on the knoll opposite Longs Park in Lancaster, where a toy store is now (1995) located. The sky was the limit! Why not insure ourselves beyond property and vehicle liability? Why not have a Lancaster Conference hospitalization plan?

Boshart Wins Day For Mennonite Mutual Aid

When Lloyd Boshart, in charge of Mennonite Mutual Aid in the eastern United States, heard about the possibility of a second health plan, Mennonite Mutual Aid decided to press its case again. This time MMA took off the kid gloves. In person, Lloyd Boshart called MMA officers, Orie Miller and Abram Hallman, to tell them about this issue. With their blessing he drove to Salunga, where the Bishop Board had recently begun to meet since the mission board had enlarged its facilities.

Lloyd was granted a session with the Bishop Board. Paul Landis, its young secretary, noted that Lloyd made clear that Mennonite Mutual Aid "gives assistance on a brotherhood basis to special needs...It is not intended to be an insurance company." This pro-brotherhood language made sense even to people generally suspicious of Mennonite organizations in Goshen, Indiana. But Boshart's presentation touched another good chord, the congrega-tion. "In the congregation plan," he explained, "if a minimum of forty percent of the members are involved then no one is considered ineligible because of health conditions."

Stoner Krady and Elmer Martin, both turning 70 years old (and still on the Bishop Board, although Stoner had resigned from the Brotherly Aid Sponsoring Committee), must have been pleased with the clarity of that point.

But Boshart saved his trump card till last: "Mennonite Mutual Aid has over 27,000 members and 1,000 of them are Lancaster Conference adults." One thousand!

Lutz Tips Balance to Mennonite Mutual Aid

The bishops drew a collective breath. They knew that 1,000 meant one in every fifteen members of Lancaster Conference. Almost seven percent, rules or no rules. And how many others besides Earl Groff had coverage by employ-ers? There might even be one or two Mennonite Mutual Aid plans lurking among the bishops.

The discussion moved fast. One hand shot up. A bishop asked what the Industrial Relations Committee had come up with in the year and a half since the bishops asked them to work on this. Heads turned to Frank Enck who was on the committee. "Nothing to show," he replied. So without further ado the bishops elected one of their own, Clarence Lutz, to join the study committee. They knew when a committee needed a businessman to help get something done.

Clarence Lutz, the progressive (by 1960s standards) bishop of the Elizabethtown district and owner of a thriving fuel oil business with his name on it, pressed forward. He knew what employers were expected to provide for employees in those days. In the eleven months after the Boshart appeal, the study committee held a special meeting with the chair of Mennonite Mutual Aid and surveyed all 130 congregations of the conference.

By December 1964, the Bishop Board approved establishing "an office for hospitalization for our conference and to give further study to coordination

Clarence Lutz was appointed to the Hospitalization Study Committee and was significant in bringing resolution to the question of hospitalization and medical benefits.

of Brotherly Aid in our conference," and in a separate action "to appoint John Shenk as secretary for hospitalization if he is willing to accept this."

The more traditional people sighed in relief at that action. They thought they had kept the denominational church offices at Goshen at bay once again. The people hoping for change trembled, fearing another Lancaster Conference entrenchment in isolationism. Paul Landis, the secretary of conference at that time, remembers years later that, in many ways, it was not a great moment, not a big crisis.

"Our people would trust a local address," Paul recalls. "If we did nothing it would mean letting Mennonite Mutual Aid have its way. Remember, at that time Lancaster Mennonite Conference was not a part of General Conference, so we had no official voice in Mennonite Mutual Aid."

Unlike the 1939 attempt by Orie Miller to establish a mutual aid plan for the mission board, this time, a full quarter of a century later, the institutions had their hands on the helm of the conference ship. The mission board had just built a new wing and was looking for tenants to fill its empty offices until it could occupy them. The institutions spawned in the past decade of the conference, now responsible for over 200 employees, were looking for a way to settle the medical plan issue.

And here were the new leaders of conference employing a new decision-making tool, a questionnaire. The study committee sent out 190 questionnaires on May 22, 1964. Paul Burkholder at Glad Tidings congregation in New York City returned his first, urging the committee to move forward. His positive reaction forecast the tone for nearly all the rest. At Oak Shade Mennonite Church, Ray Yost reported that of the seven working families "four have no coverage and all seven are interested in a conference program." James Rheam of Cobbtown, Florida reported that medical coverage is "very much needed in this area, as insurance companies seem to be capitalizing on so many and then not paying when the need arises." Paul H. Weaver of the Metzler congregation wrote that "it would be ideal to have such aid in our own conference since the hospital rates are becoming higher all the time." Monroe Peifer summed up most of the sentiment in his brief report from Atmore, Alabama: "We need something."

The questionnaire touched a still sensitive nerve for those who expressed mutual care in older forms: Leonard Brunk, writing from the West Union congregation, noted that "there is some concern that we don't come to rely on things such as this and lose the blessing of personally helping each other." And from John Shenk's home congregation, East Petersburg, Norman Landis wrote: "Personally I do not want to criticize this idea of having such protection, because there are those who have benefited by it. But on the other hand, I feel we are losing our trust in our all-knowing heavenly Father and in many areas are looking to the plans of man to satisfy our needs." He admitted that the congregation had no plan for meeting the medical, hospitalization, and burial expenses of needy members. The members who were able and chose to have insurance at East Petersburg, as Landis reported, relied on Banker's Life, Hartford Company, American Progressive, Connecticut General, Reading-American Casualty Company, Blue Cross, and Mennonite Aid.

All summer the replies trickled back to Ivan Leaman. Finally 109 returned with nearly as many positive replies. When in December 1964 the decision was made to establish an office, Paul Landis could confidently report that "there is good response to the poll of our conference members regarding hospitalization plan. There are now," he said to the 26-member Bishop Board of the conference, "more than enough affirmative votes to give approval to establishing an office for hospitalization for our conference."

Now should the conference ask its own Brotherly Aid to develop a medical plan? Or should the Mennonite Mutual Aid medical plan be customized, with an office that the conference itself would staff?

It could have gone either way. The worst fears of the progressives did not materialize. Lancaster Conference had a plan, but it was a Mennonite Mutual Aid plan customized for the local people. It was probably Clarence Lutz who swayed it in the direction of Mennonite Mutual Aid. His friendliness to Mennonite Mutual Aid was recognized by Mennonite Mutual Aid. In November 1966, Mennonite Mutual Aid invited him to Chicago as a "specially invited guest" to the first Mennonite Mutual Aid Association meeting.

At this time, just three years before the 1968 conservative separation, the progressives were becoming tired of always holding back for fear of offending the conservative wing. On the Mennonite Mutual Aid front they were determined to go the way of most other Mennonite conferences.

New Conference Leadership Guides Brotherly Aid

By 1965, the hand of a new generation of conference leaders was evident in these actions. Gone were the days of 1939 when the conference was as ambiguous about overseas missions as it was suspicious of insurance. Gone the days when an Elmer Martin could publish an article in *Pastoral Messenger* on how overseas missions can lead to erosion of doctrine.

Here in the brand-new 1964 was a new Bishop Board moderator, David Thomas, 45 years old; a new secretary of conference, Paul Landis; John Shenk; Frank Enck (treasurer of conference); H. Raymond Charles (bishop of Landisville district and president of the mission board); Paul Dagen in the south, 40 years old; and Howard Witmer, 39 years old, waiting in the wings. In the amen corner now sat Stoner and Elmer seeing life in its later stages.

Stoner must have mused that of the five officers of conference in 1965 he had ordained two, David Thomas and Frank Enck. A third, Simon Bucher, had been his protégé in the Brotherly Aid work.

The twin mutual aid plans now were triplets: Hospital Aid joined Fire and Storm and Liability for autos.

Hospitalization and Liability set up housekeeping at Salunga. Fire and Storm, though, stayed in Raymond Sauder's kitchen a few more years.

Mennonite Mutual Aid staff at MMA headquarters in Goshen, Indiana. Mennonite Mutual Aid and Sharing Programs have worked cooperatively in a variety of ways over the years. Until recent years, John Shenk served as a representative in Pennsylvania for MMA's health and hospitalization plan. The Sharing Programs office has serviced membership and claims in Pennsylvania for Mennonite Automobile Aid, Inc. Sharing Programs and Mennonite Mutual Aid are both members of the Association of Mennonite Aid Societies.

— *Chapter 12* —

Mennonite Brotherly Aid Office Opens

In April 1965, the Brotherly Aid Liability Plan and the hospitalization program opened a single-room office in the mission board's building in Salunga, Pennsylvania. The telephone number for the hospitalization program was 898-8541, it was announced at the next Brotherly Aid board meeting. Mennonite Brotherly Aid was chosen as the name for the office handling the hospitalization. John Shenk agreed to serve part-time. Now he and Myrtle knew they could reclaim the Brotherly Aid Liability Plan space at home for themselves and their children.

Landis Tidies Up Conference Administration

These changes had come fairly quickly. Clarence Lutz and Paul Landis kept the Bishop Board abreast of all the details. By the third-to-last day of 1964, Paul Landis was able to write a memo to his fellow officers of conference, explaining that "John Shenk has given an affirmative answer to our request for him to give leadership to the Hospitalization Plan." He went on to note that John was working for the Provident Bookstore one-quarter time and one-sixth time for the Brotherly Aid Liability Plan. (Myrtle worked almost the same time for the Brotherly Aid Liability Plan as he did.) The rest of his working time went to his duties as pastor. John later would be willing to quit his work at the bookstore and give four days a week to the Hospitalization and Brotherly Aid Liability Plans.

Paul took the occasion of that memo to again chide the Bishop Board for (1) not listing the Brotherly Aid Plan and the Brotherly Aid Liability Plan in the conference committee listing and (2) not regularly appointing members to those committees. He could have said the same about appointing members to the Brotherly Aid Sponsoring Committee itself. As far as Paul could tell, those members appointed 14 years ago were on for life.

Administrative contacts with Paul Landis, the youngest bishop on record and the first to be "employed" as an officer of conference, helped John Shenk understand his new role. As leader at the new Hospitalization Plan office, John mediated among Mennonite Mutual Aid in Goshen (where he had 12 years before walked the sidewalks as a student at Goshen College), the individuals who enrolled, and the congregations that enrolled by congregational plan. He used Mennonite Mutual Aid literature with a local stamp on it, deleting sections that did not apply.

As the young, new Lancaster Conference administrators understood it, the conference had responded to a new issue with a new administrative entity, a new office, and staff people. The new office also helped to fill the empty space in the expanded mission board headquarters in Salunga. But, of course, the Brotherly Aid Sponsoring Committee had been officially functioning since 1949, and the "staff" had been paid since 1950. Since 1950, there had been office space in homes.

Paul Landis, secretary of the Bishop Board since 1962, began in earnest to put the conference administrative house in order. Once he assumed staff duties, Paul urged the conference to declare itself regarding its commitment to Brotherly Aid: Are the Plans part of conference or are they not? Does his work as secretary of conference involve any oversight of Brotherly Aid Sponsoring Committee appointments?

After the 1965 New Year lull, Paul, with the help of his secretary, Betty Gerber, was ready in early February to plunge ahead and put the question to the bishops. He proposed in writing that the Hospitalization Plan be declared "an official program under the Lancaster Conference" and that it come under the Brotherly Aid "Sponsoring Committee," that had first been appointed in 1949. The informal state of administration had left it unclear to Paul whether Stoner Krady was still a member, although Clair Eby, Krady's replacement, was listed as a member.

He proposed that the Bishop Board give "definite terms of office to those who are appointed." In effect he was proposing the reorganization of the Brotherly Aid Sponsoring Committee, giving it a fresh start on good footing in the conference family of organizations, what the bishops had just done to their own house in the early 1960s. His administrative work as VS director had given him a taste of the basics of organizational structure.

Spring conference was just around the corner, and Paul hoped to settle this soon. The third week of March 1965 the Bishop Board made a sweeping change in the relationship between the Brotherly Aid Plans and the church. In a full page of Bishop Board minutes Paul, with David Thomas as moderator, led the Bishop Board to state unequivocally that the Brotherly Aid Fire and Storm Plan and the Brotherly Aid Liability Plan "be officially recognized by conference" and that the "committee now known as the Brotherly Aid Sponsoring Committee henceforth be known as the Brotherly Aid Board of the LMC." That board was defined as having nine members. It was to elect its officers annually and make an annual report to conference through the Bishop Board. The official Bishop Board minute went on to state that the Hospitalization Plan, along with the other two Plans, would operate under the new board.[53]

This action was astonishing in several regards. First, the Bishop Board had already approved and appointed the Brotherly Aid Sponsoring Committee in 1949. Second, the Hospitalization Plan was really an MMA plan and could not "operate under" a second board. It seems ironic that it was first Brotherly Aid that sought a home in the Conference and was now being told that its home had to be in Conference.

No sooner had the 26 bishops present passed this action, than Stoner Krady, now living in Philadelphia, who had helped give birth to the organized plan 17 years earlier, took the floor. He bemoaned "the lack of concern and involvement in our conference in Jewish evangelism." The 1940s and 1950s old guard had indeed moved on!

He had lived to see a new generation enlarge and refine the work that he had begun by charisma and bridge-building among an earlier generation of bishops. He hardly participated in the pivotal discussions of 1965. By Thanksgiving Day of the following year he would preach his last sermon, suffer a stroke that evening and die the next day, moving on to the ultimate realm of mutual life. His efforts in starting the Brotherly Aid Plans would be remembered as only a secondary role behind his evangelism activities.

Reorganized Board Meets

On July 10, 1965, the reorganized Brotherly Aid board met at Salunga. Andrew Shaub, James Hess, Elmer Martin, Clair Eby, and Simon Bucher continued from the previous Sponsoring Committee. Four new members joined: Edwin Gehman, Monroe Garber, Ivan Charles, Jr., and Alvin Weaver. With a new title, a clarified relationship to conference, and a new mandate to oversee three plans, this freshly minted group took decisive action: to get their telephone number listed; to invite a member of each plan to attend the board meetings; to make quarterly reports; to approve a letterhead; and to request a reporting slot at the fall conference.

Although the board tabled the issue of the type and extent of the "study and teaching on the general brotherly aid theme," it did, by request of the Bishop Board, study the new Medicare program and declare that it is just "a part of the Social Security program" for people over 65 years old.

With John Shenk making this a regular staff duty, the Brotherly Aid board leapt ahead on many fronts. It agreed to accept no more out-of-state Brotherly Aid Liability Plan agreements after November 1965. In this matter state boundaries superseded conference boundaries because of "increasing legal and administrative complications."

A large $39,000 Brotherly Aid Liability Plan claim loomed on the horizon. Andrew Shaub, board chair, and the BALP officers approached Clarence Harnish, chairman of the Fire and Storm Plan general committee, for a large short-term loan. The Fire and Storm committee declined. Although one and the same board gave oversight to the two Plans, the two programs continued to function independently. Mutual aid among the Plans themselves was still on a distant horizon.

John Shenk, newly empowered by sufficient time and the office services of the mission board surrounding him, carefully but rapidly urged the Brotherly Aid board to reflect its high calling. He brought Association of Mennonite Aid Societies (AMAS) booklets to the board's attention ("Why Christians Help One Another" and "Toward a Theology of Servanthood"). He attended churchwide meetings of Mennonite Mutual Aid at Laurelville and Chicago, taking along with him as many board members as possible. A brochure was planned for distribution. His seminary learning helped him envision the central place mutuality could have in the church.[54]

Eighteen years after J. Winfield Fretz's booklet came into James Hess's hands and stirred him to organize mutual aid, Brotherly Aid was again getting back to verbalizing its mission.

Cooperation With Mennonite Mutual Aid Grows

The wall between conference and the Indiana-based Mennonite Mutual Aid came down completely in 1966. The Bishop Board allowed the Brotherly Aid Liability Plan to work cooperatively with Mennonite Mutual Aid so people could have in one package Mennonite Automobile Aid's collision/comprehensive coverage and Brotherly Aid Liability Plan's liability. After that, as new Mennonite Mutual Aid services came, such as Mennonite Foundation, Lancaster Conference usually did not raise cautions.

In these early years of Brotherly Aid at Salunga, John Shenk made quarterly reports on the Brotherly Aid Liability and Hospitalization plans. Fire and Storm reports were not very forthcoming. Usually it took a telephone call to Clarence Harnish, and then a few numbers were given to the board.

Hospitalization grew steadily after the Salunga office opened. In October 1966, John Shenk told the board that he served 1,950 Lancaster Conference members. By May 1967, John counted 2,362 persons of Lancaster Conference in the four available health plans. Most chose the Comprehensive Health Plan.

By March 1973, 2,628 Lancaster Conference members (7.9 percent of all Mennonite Mutual Aid members and 16.7 percent of Lancaster Conference membership) were enrolled in Mennonite Mutual Aid health plans. Forty-two congregations had appointed congregational representatives. John had visited 45 congregations to talk about the plans. John was becoming Mr. Brotherly Aid.

Hospitalization was a child of Lancaster Conference since conference owned its office and staff. Hospitalization was also a stepchild of Lancaster Conference since Mennonite Mutual Aid owned the plan. Hospitalization continued to serve under the umbrella of Brotherly Aid until Mennonite Mutual Aid set up its own office in the Lancaster area in 1975. Since then Brotherly Aid's work in processing medical coverage has practically disappeared.

— Chapter 13 —

Mennonite Brotherly Aid Office Prospers

The Hospitalization Plan came as a comet in the Lancaster Conference firmament—brilliant while it lasted, with a tail of secondary effects larger than itself. Because of the coming of the Hospitalization Plan:

- The Brotherly Aid board was reorganized and taken seriously by the rest of the conference organizations.

- Conference finally and fully adopted and renewed its covenant with the existing plans in language understood by the new generation.

- The Brotherly Aid work no longer lived secluded on someone's porch but became public in its own office.

- The Brotherly Aid plans received more visibility in the church, including listing in the conference directory and reports at conference.

- Brotherly Aid created full-time positions.

- Brotherly Aid people began to attend Mennonite Mutual Aid delegate meetings.

- People embraced more fully the Mennonite Mutual Aid mission in the church, giving and receiving counsel from a larger circle of people, which led the way to the conference accepting partnership with other churchwide-based programs.

But comets soon trail off to distant realms.

With the busily growing mission board office around the small beachhead that Brotherly Aid had established at Salunga, and with John's leadership, the daily work became more predictable and mathematical. The paperwork became more routine. The onslaught of loss claims became more manageable and less spontaneous. Yet the conviction of sharing instead of insurance showed through stronger than ever in the annual reports.

John Shenk Workload Increases

Although he was no longer alone, John began to wonder if his tasks had multiplied beyond his capacity to fulfill them. By now he was also working a few hours per week at Menno Housing in addition to fulfilling his Brotherly Aid responsibilities.

Ivan Leaman met with him weekly at the office. On John's 37th birthday, June 5, 1967, the day the Six Day War broke out in Israel, Lloyd Zeager began to work in the Mennonite Brotherly Aid office full-time. Lloyd, a young fellow from the Strickler Mennonite Church, was the only boy in his high school class to major in secretarial courses.

Paul N. Kraybill, in his function as personnel manager of the mission board, had asked Lloyd if he would work there. Lloyd was getting tired and bored of pushing logs through his father's sawmill. So Lloyd accepted Kraybill's offer. He worked at Mennonite Brotherly Aid until he went to Goshen College in the fall of 1972.

In November 1967, John, along with several board members, visited the Mennonite Mutual Aid offices in Goshen, Indiana. He saw the new IBM equipment that "makes it possible to handle the bookkeeping very efficiently by machine," he told his board.[55] On return to their modest typewriter presided over by Lloyd Zeager, John began to put the assessments for the health plans straight through to Goshen.

One day in 1968 while Lloyd was typing, John stood up to put something in the cabinet and fell to the floor. Lloyd, hearing the fall, thought it might be a heart attack. The receptionist who sat immediately outside the Brotherly Aid door made a call for help. When John regained his senses, he was in an ambulance on the way to a hospital in Lancaster City.[56]

An old physical problem had come back to haunt John. His bishop, Raymond Charles, who was also president of the mission board and in the office part-time each week, started to suspect that John was working too hard. After chatting to a few people about John's workload, Raymond finally told John to take a two-week break.

After the break, John was even more convinced that something had to be done about the workload. Yet it was hard to give up tasks to others. After Lloyd respectfully asked if there was anything he could do to lighten the burden, John began to give him simple tasks in the Hospitalization Plan. Yet it was some time until Lloyd took over most of that work.

For a while John talked with Ray Geigley about working at the office. But Ray found other employment. Later, it looked as if the deacon at

Rawlinsville, where Stoner Krady had cut his teeth on property administration, H. Elvin Herr, would take some of the burden off John.

But little help materialized. His quarterly reports to the board became more insistent that he needed help.

State Challenges Liability Plan

One early November morning in 1967, John noticed in the stack of incoming mail a sober-looking brown envelope from the Insurance Department of Pennsylvania. With apprehension he sat down to open it. In blunt, terse, yet cordial bureaucratic language, directed personally to John, it said that "it has been brought to the attention of our department that your association is transacting the business of insurance in the Commonwealth of Pennsylvania without being licensed by this department." Richard Krimm, the deputy insurance commissioner, set a time for a meeting.

The Brotherly Aid Liability Plan had just recently enrolled its 3,000th vehicle. Two weeks earlier the plan completed its 13th year of business. Could the number "13" possibly bring woe? What would the state, or at least the Republican administration of Governor Raymond Schafer, want with this small religious group? And how did they find out about it?

On Tuesday morning, November 28, 1967, the veteran administrative committee (Edwin, Ivan, and John) had a prayer and traveled west on Route 230, arriving at the Insurance Department building at 10:30 a.m. Mr. Krimm was in another meeting, so they were seen by Mr. Kuntz, director of the Bureau of Companies of the department.

Mr. Kuntz received the three plain-coated, ordained men cordially, sat them down across the desk from himself, cleared his throat, and asked them to explain the Brotherly Aid Liability Plan. He focused not on the administrative details of the Plan but on who could join. On his desk the fat volume of insurance laws lay open to the section about exceptions for religious organizations. Kuntz was candid and sympathetic, admitting that in a sense Pennsylvania would like to have the Brotherly Aid Liability Plan under its jurisdiction. That way the state could feel that it was in control of the auto liability situation, which at that time was a jungle of claims. Yet he was willing to defend the Brotherly Aid Liability Plan's religious exemptions.

Two things, he noted, could force the Brotherly Aid Liability Plan under state control: (1) extending membership outside church boundaries and (2) failing to meet liability obligations. The three sat still, memorizing what he said.

Beside Kuntz's law books lay some other papers. From that stack he lifted up a current Brotherly Aid Liability Plan financial statement. After a bit of scrutiny he said, "How can we criticize the kind of job you have done?"

By 1995, nearly 200 persons were involved as representatives for BALP and Fire/Storm Plans. Here Jane Hartzler is orienting Clara and Donald Stoner to their new role as BALP representatives.

Ivan, the treasurer, must have felt a warm, secular blessing with those words, and relaxed a bit. But Edwin and John, in the midst of this compliment, were suddenly chilled to the bone. When Mr. Kuntz lifted up the financial statement, they couldn't help noticing a Brotherly Aid Liability Plan annual statement and its cover letter. Mr. Kuntz said nothing about how these Brotherly Aid Liability Plan reports had come into the hands of the Insurance Department.

Someone who received one must have sent it. Was it a member of the Plan keeping Harrisburg bureaucrats informed? Was there a mole in the membership? Did the Association of Mennonite Aid Societies send it? Was Lloyd Hershey's 1949 question about how it would look to have two plans in the church coming back to haunt them?

Mr. Kuntz expressed no alarm. He seemed to understand the goals of the Brotherly Aid Liability Plan and he expressed sympathy with the philosophy. He noted the high degree of Mennonite Church loyalty and observed that "in light of the philosophy and goals of the brotherhood you should actually have one hundred percent participation on the part of your church."

This was an admonition that all three men received with gratitude. The Brotherly Aid Liability Plan membership numbered just 2,000 out of a potential field of membership ten times that number.

Before the session in Harrisburg closed, Mr. Kuntz required nothing to change in order for the Brotherly Aid Liability Plan to continue as it had been, but he made four suggestions:

- Register Brotherly Aid Liability Plan with the state, which would not involve any state control.

- Get reinsurance for extremely high claims.

- Invest funds rather than keep them dormant in a bank.

- Get a security bond with the state rather than making security deposits for each claim.

In 90 minutes the visit was over. The men ate lunch and drove back to Salunga where they had parked their cars. John felt that the visit had clarified the Brotherly Aid Liability Plan's relationship to the state, and he felt eager to clarify Brotherly Aid's own purpose of existence—and maybe his personal purpose with the Plan. But he knew that anything the Brotherly Aid Liability Plan did from now on might be known by the Commonwealth.

Fire and Storm Grows, Independent of State

While the Liability Plan was on the agenda in Harrisburg, the Fire and Storm Plan, the "elder brother" plan, mailed out assessments to its 2,290 participants, many having more than one agreement. The Fire and Storm Plan was covering a total valuation of $84 million in property. Phoebe Ann Sauder, daughter of Plan treasurer Raymond Sauder, did the staff work, since her father's health was declining.

Fire and Storm work seemed simple compared to the Liability Plan work. Fire and Storm did not have to contend with legal actions from claimants or worry about intrusions by the state in its work. After 17 years Clarence Harnish, chair, was still preparing the annual report. Raymond Sauder was only the second treasurer for the Plan. Melvin Graybill was the second secretary, following Roy Ulrich.

Fire and Storm was facing large coverage requests from organizations such as Landis Homes and Victor Weaver, Inc. Enrolling such large properties required special action by the Brotherly Aid Board. The general committee used a guideline limiting enrollment to properties with values no more than four mills (4/1000) of the total valuation of the Plan. The committee felt uneasy with such large properties because they could potentially consume a large portion of the funds available for all the properties enrolled. The requests, accompanied by persuasive appeals to be a part of the Fire and Storm Plan, prompted the committee to find some unheard-of "bedfellows." To honor the desire of the property owners, the committee agreed to share coverage of property and contents with other coverage providers. Sometimes the "bedfellows" were Mennonite-related organizations such as Tri-County Mutual or Mennonite Mutual of Intercourse (Lloyd Hershey's company). And sometimes Fire & Storm shared coverage with Old Guard or Reamstown Mutual.

The general committee had some other new decisions to make also. Sometimes the question of damages indirectly related to fires and storms required judgment calls. And in 1969, a large loss at the Hollinger Farm Market prompted the Brotherly Aid board to divide properties into risk categories and vary the assessment accordingly.

While Fire and Storm had to adapt to its members' needs, there were no state "eyes" watching. But state regulations were forcing the Liability Plan to have a strong central organization.

In 1968, a block of conservative-minded persons left Lancaster Conference to form their own conference. Much of the strongest resistance to Mennonite Mutual Aid went with them. John, in giving the Hospitalization Plan annual report six months after the departure of the conservatives, forthrightly stated at the East Chestnut Street afternoon meeting that this plan "is a part of Mennonite Mutual Aid."

The new outward-looking spirit of conference extended not only to the west and Mennonite Mutual Aid, but also to the east, in Africa. Fraternal visits with people from Africa influenced Brotherly Aid. When the Brotherly Aid annual meeting closed, it was Pastor Nashon K. Nyambok of Tanzania who led the closing prayer.

"We are living in an age of paradoxes," John reported, speaking for the office in Salunga, completing its fourth year of operation as Mennonite Brotherly Aid. "One of these paradoxes is that in spite of our abundance and means at our disposal for various types of material assistance, there are individuals in our congregations and communities [here he thought of people in Pastor Nyambok's church] who either do not have access to this abundance or are frustrated by the channels though which assistance is available. As brothers and sisters in Christ we cannot neglect our responsibility to one another if we are really caring Christians."

John Requests Help Again

In June 1968 John had felt ready to appeal to the Brotherly Aid board for help again. He had asked "to be relieved of a major portion of the administrative responsibilities he was now carrying in the office." The board authorized him and Larry Newswanger, the office manager at the mission board, to search for a staff person. "If my services are needed," John wrote to the

Pastor Nashon K. Nyambok and his family.
Pastor Nyambok led the closing prayer at the
1968 Annual Meeting of the Brotherly Aid plans.

board in June 1968, "I am willing to continue responsibility for the handling of Brotherly Aid Liability Plan and MAA. Beyond this I do not see myself being available for more than a counseling or advisory role." He hoped an assistant would be in the office by the end of July.

Yet by October rather than another staff person John had another assignment: to plan a major review of the Brotherly Aid Liability Plan as it approached its 14th anniversary.

The 14-Year Review

The review was held at Salunga 9:30 to 3:00 March 29, 1969. With Ivan Leaman moderating, it opened with James Hess giving a devotional meditation entitled, "Christian Mutual Aid" (also the title of the Fretz booklet). Then Edwin Gehman gave a review of the Brotherly Aid Liability Plan before John came onto the scene. Then John, until the noon meal, would speak one and a half hours about the current state of the Plan.

The "invited resource person" was Edgar Stoesz, president of Goodville Mutual Casualty Company. For all the importance the board attached to a review, only 37 persons showed up. John was especially sorry that more local representatives did not come. The group concluded that the Plan was doing fine, but needed to remind people that it is not insurance.

In his report to the board, John wrote that he hoped that by September 1969 he would have office help so that Lloyd Zeager and Elvin Herr could manage the Hospitalization Plan and John and a secretary could manage the Liability Plan. He noted that MMA's Comprehensive Health Plan quarterly assessments were going to rise from $25 to $28, a decision made, he noted, with considerable soul-searching.

Office Secretary Hired

This time John's wish came true. Barbara Keller began work September 15, 1969, as John's secretary for the Brotherly Aid Liability Plan. "I expect to be able to handle the administration of the program somewhat more adequately than I have in the past," John told the board shortly after Barbara started. She remained with the Plans until 1975.

After ten years on the job, joy was creeping back into John's work. This year the board would put him on full-time pay ($449 a month) with all the time off for pastoring he wanted. Along with the mission board staff, he received medical coverage and retirement.

Yet as a pastor, it puzzled him that "our young people and possibly most of their parents think of their needs in this area as business needs rather than brotherhood needs," he pondered to the board. "The question of whether or not this program continues to be a legitimate one depends in part on whether or not a sense of Christian brotherhood and responsibility can be kept alive among us."

Business, indeed!

Car Power Pricks Consciences and Prices

Detroit thought it knew what the car business was in 1969—raw power and conquest. In December 1969 the Brotherly Aid Liability Plan sent out to its 35 representatives this list of cars not eligible for the Brotherly Aid Liability Plan: Camaro Z/28, Cougar Eliminator, Corvette, Dodge Hemi, Mustang Boss, Plymouth Hemi, and Shelby Cobra. These were cars, not computer games!

Another 36 models were eligible to enroll if the engines were under 350 CID (cubic inch displacement). However, the letter to representatives about high-performance cars noted, "if the local representative learns that a car does not have a stock engine he shall report the details of the customization to the secretary and inform the participant that his enrollment is subject to the approval of the administrative committee."

These were the days the United States was charging into Vietnam and

Thailand, and Americans were charging around in cars named after weapons (Javelin), fierce animals (Super Bee, Barracuda, Cobra, Road Runner, Firebird), natural disasters (Cyclone Spoiler), etc.

New Decade Beckons

The curtain of the 1960s decade came down the afternoon of November 11, 1969, at the Bowmansville Mennonite Church. During that annual meeting Clarence Harnish, now 65 years old, announced that Vernon Charles had become treasurer of the Fire and Storm Plan. Raymond Sauder was not well but had the strength to say that he is "thankful to the Great Healer for his grace during this affliction."[57] His affliction would soon end his life.

Clarence used his report time also to reappoint all local committee members for additional three-year terms, supposedly whether they wanted it or not. Brotherly Aid people were beginning to notice an administrative style gap between the Fire and Storm Plan and the reorganized Brotherly Aid board.

John Shenk gave the Brotherly Aid Liability Plan report and then the Mennonite Brotherly Aid office report, which by now referred to the Mennonite Mutual Aid medical plans and the Mennonite Automobile Aid, Inc. (MAAI) collision/comprehensive program. On the eve of the new decade he brought an omen of how medical expenses would plague the future generations. He told the crowd at Bowmansville that, while an average cost per day in the hospital in 1946 was $9.39, "Today [1969]," he said, "the average cost is $70 per day." Statisticians had stopped counting cents years ago.

According to secretary Elmer Martin, Jr., son of a founding board member, the Brotherly Aid people "were thankful for the goodly number" at the meeting. John felt renewed in spirit to work for the Plan. Young Vernon Charles was eager to take responsibility at his large farmhouse office. Barbara Keller was in the office; Elvin Herr, in the field. When Benjamin Weaver blew through the D hole of his pitch pipe and led the congregation in "Blessed Assurance," it surely seemed to all involved that the reports of the plans were indeed "a foretaste of glory divine."

This 1923 Model T Ford, owned by Allen and Mabel Martin, is the oldest car enrolled in the Brotherly Aid Liability Plan.

— *Chapter 14* —

No-fault Law Forces a Choice

Assurance was blessed. Insurance, though, was another matter.

Only four agenda items into the new decade and John dropped a Brotherly Aid Liability Plan bombshell. In this quarter, he wrote in his report to the board, the average cost per claim settlement jumped from $400 to $500. The statistic rang with the dulling reality of inflation and the end of the American post-World War II economic boom. In a few more quarters, $500 would look like the horse and buggy days.

The mission board's Voluntary Service director, Larry Newswanger, brought a request that Brotherly Aid find a way for VSers in inner-city assignments to cover personal property theft losses.

Not passed. Buildings are one thing. Stereos and bell-bottom blue jeans were, well, another.

However, another mission board administrator's request did receive a sympathetic hearing early in 1970. A Mennonite owned a piece of property next to Glad Tidings Mennonite Church in New York City. His insurance had been canceled by a commercial company because it was located "in a ghetto community." Would the church adjust to the urban situation and respond to this need? Would the church see it as closely akin to the original 1948 intent of Brotherly Aid—to help protect church property? Paul Landis brought a proposal to extend Brotherly Aid coverage to this property. It was accepted. But it was labeled as an exception to the rule.

The relief that Barbara Keller had brought to John was insufficient by 1970, with the slow but steady increase of members. By May 1970 John again requested help. Just keeping the bookkeeping up-to-date was hard enough, but practically nothing could be done by way of promotion and education about mutual aid as a tenet of faith. Elvin Herr said he couldn't spend much time as a field worker for the health plans.

Mennonite Mutual Aid Health Plan Grows and Adapts

In light of the growth of the Hospitalization Plan in Lancaster Conference and with an eye toward the future, Harold Swartzentruber, executive secretary of Mennonite Mutual Aid, requested a meeting to talk over matters with the Brotherly Aid board.

Harold met with the board on October 23, 1970. Board members Andrew Shaub, James Hess, Edwin Gehman, Alvin Sauder, David Buckwalter, Monroe Garber, Ivan Charles, and Elmer Martin, Jr., attended. Also present were John Shenk, Lloyd Zeager, and Paul Musser, who was considering a position with Brotherly Aid. Mennonite Mutual Aid board member Abram Hallman was there too.

Harold recounted the beginning of Mennonite Mutual Aid with a hospital plan in 1950. Currently (1970) Mennonite Mutual Aid had 35,000 members, an enormous increase from the 16,000 that Boshart reported in 1964. In one year the assessments for the medical plans totaled $3.5 million. He expressed appreciation for the good work that John and Lloyd were doing.[58]

"When we compare ourselves...with the insurance industry, we have every reason to feel like amateurs," John noted in 1970. "However, in the day by day work...there are times when I sense that, after all, the Lord may be wanting to use this 'weak vessel' to demonstrate a style of Christian dependence from which we so often shy away."

By fall 1970, pressures were still on and John raised the idea of renting a computer. No action. The first computer would come to Brotherly Aid in 1976.

John Requests More Help

Finally, on April 21, 1971, John threw down the gauntlet, telling the board to get help or else. "In previous meetings," he informed them, "I have already taken too much of your time discussing my personal and organizational frustrations in relation to the plan without providing the leadership to keep moving in meaningful direction." He went on to insist that they move "deliberately but promptly" toward decisions to avoid "catastrophe either personally or organizationally or both."

His honeymoon as director of the office was definitely over. He had lost a personal sense of fulfillment. He recommended that Edgar Stoesz come to a review meeting as a consultant. "I will likewise," he concluded in his plea to the board, "need to make a definite decision whether I can commit myself with enthusiasm to the direction which is taken or whether for my own well-being and of the Plan, I need to move on to something else."

The valiant young director who rescued a kitchen-table operation in 1960 was now asking it to rescue him.

Early 1970s Brings Changes

The early 1970s were watershed years for all three Brotherly Aid plans. The years 1972-75 saw the Fire and Storm Plan engage its first staff person,

Vernon Charles, as a field worker; Hospitalization turned the future over to Larry Newswanger at the new Mennonite Mutual Aid regional office on Greenfield Road, Lancaster, Pennsylvania; and the Brotherly Aid Liability Plan moved to larger quarters and made the shift to no-fault insurance laws.

Of those three events the one that tried the very soul the most was the state laws concerning insurance that went into effect in 1975. In short, liability coverage became compulsory and the Pennsylvania Supreme Court quickly upheld its constitutionality.

The Brotherly Aid Liability Plan had plenty of time to anticipate some kind of change. As early as 1971 John Shenk sent out the warning shot, going on record that the Brotherly Aid Liability Plan would need to consider the issue sometime. Anyone, of course, who read the newspapers could have known this. For at least four years the issue periodically made front pages and became a hot potato in election years. This was the case in most of the states of the union.

During this period all people concerned with auto liability were trying to read the political winds blowing in Harrisburg. This climatic change produced a spin-off industry: insurance consultants. The Brotherly Aid Liability Plan engaged the services of Neal Dubson of Lansdowne, Pennsylvania. Depending on the latest omens divined by the soothsayers, there were times the Brotherly Aid Liability Plan had little hope of surviving.

Brotherly Aid Liability Plan Considers Options

Mr. Kuntz of the Pennsylvania Insurance Department met again with the Brotherly Aid Liability Plan team in 1971 and said it looked like three choices would be available: self-insurance, fraternal beneficiary society, or a group insurance plan.

Edgar Stoesz, a colleague of Brotherly Aid Board member Monroe Garber (also a board member of and agent for Goodville), offered to rescue the Brotherly Aid Liability Plan from this new law by the latter option.

On June 22, 1973, Edgar proposed that the Brotherly Aid Liability Plan transfer everything to Goodville, lock, stock and barrel, and begin to "serve as a Goodville agency."

"Goodville would assume your entire book of business," he wrote, sensing an opportunity both to rescue a poor cousin and to substantially increase Goodville's welfare. He estimated that as a group plan under Goodville, the Brotherly Aid Liability Plan could expect a commission income of $50,000 a year. With that commission the Brotherly Aid Liability Plan would have to run its operation as a group plan under Goodville. To sweeten the package even more, Stoesz offered that Brotherly Aid could select one

Goodville board member. "We already value the services of numerous Lancaster Conference members on the board of directors and in the staff," he noted in his proposal to the Brotherly Aid Liability Plan.[59]

Later that year, in September, a special meeting was convened to consider the options. Consultant Neal Dubson was on hand for technical advice. The original spirit of Brotherly Aid prevailed: "There was little or no support for developing a formal insurance company," Paul Musser wrote in the minutes.

No-fault Becomes Law

The Pennsylvania No-fault Motor Vehicle Insurance Act was passed in 1974, to become effective in 1975. It had provision for self-insurance. That was the good news.

The bad news was that self-insurance required providing in escrow a security deposit of $50,000 for the first vehicle and $10,000 for each additional vehicle, up to a maximum of $1 million. A self-insurer with 96 or more vehicles would have to escrow the $1 million maximum. The Liability Plan had many more than 96 vehicles!

On June 12, 1975, just weeks before this law was to go into effect, James H. Hess called a meeting to consider what to do. Again the original impulse that led to the formation of Brotherly Aid 25 years earlier prevailed: "The board members were unanimously agreed that the Brotherly Aid Liability Plan should not become an insurance company."

With this resolve of spirit to back them up, James Hess, John Shenk, Ivan Leaman, Paul Musser, and their consultant Neal Dubson met four state government officials and an Insurance Department attorney at Harrisburg on June 18, 1975. By sheer nerve and the prayers of many, Dubson proposed an alternative to posting $1 million in cash. He said the Plan was prepared to post $300,000 in cash and have the officers of the Liability Plan sign a letter of commitment for the remaining $700,000.

Would the state accept this? The officials couldn't immediately say.

On June 23, the Brotherly Aid Board met again. The state had not yet responded to the proposal. "A number of brethren admonished the group to seek the Lord's blessing and guidance through the avenue of prayer that the door might be opened for the recognition and continuation of the Plan," Paul Musser noted.

To some this scenario might appear to be church versus state or persecuted minority versus the secular majority. It might appear as a ransom Brotherly Aid Liability Plan had to pay to keep its convictions against insurance. One million dollars was no small sum to a liability organization that in its September 30, 1974 annual report had reported 3,072 members with 5,263 vehicles enrolled and that in the past year had taken in only $328,145 in assessments. So prayer was a last resort. Hands were wrung and clasped. A decision had to be made.

This time James Hess had at his side his brother-in-law, David Thomas. David stood in market the day of the first meeting in 1948, when James helped found Brotherly Aid. That butcher was now the moderator of conference, the office of last resort.

Is Plan Worth $1 Million?

Independence Day plans or not, the battle of spirit was going to be fought July 3, a year before the U.S. bicentennial, on home-field turf—Salunga. Moderator David Thomas and Secretary Howard Witmer solemnly took their seats amid the anguished and fearful Brotherly Aid board. The *ad hoc* chair was Vice Chair Bishop Clair Eby (since James Hess arrived late). Clair nodded to Ivan Charles, the layman from the Manor area, who led a prayer.

It didn't take a long time, but it was a spiritual battle. The resolve of Brotherly Aid hadn't changed, even with board member Monroe Garber also a member of Goodville's board. The board agreed to offer the state $300,000 in cash security and sign a "letter of commitment" to meet the $700,000. The Brotherly Aid Liability Plan would "seek recognition as a self-insuring entity" under the new law.

"To the state," John mused many years later, "this was small fish to fry. Putting the new no-fault law into effect was no small matter and they wanted no distraction from a church conference. So they were ready to compromise."

But governments can be unpredictable. In less than a decade, the specter of uncertainty and legal threat would again visit the Liability Plan.

On July 7, 1975, John Shenk, Paul Musser, and Ivan Leaman signed a statement that the Brotherly Aid Liability Plan "will discharge all the duties of an obligor" under the new law. The state issued a certificate of self-insurance. Now that the direction was set, the Brotherly Aid Liability Plan lifted the freeze on new members and the floodgates would soon open. As the months went by, the church came to see the value of the brave self-insurance move. From the 3,000 members at the time no-fault went into effect, membership jumped to 5,337 three years later, to 8,281 in 1981, and ten years after the watershed to 13,310 members with 20,000 vehicles enrolled.

Would the Brotherly Aid ark at Salunga be able to hold all those seeking safety?

Vernon Charles, the farmer who became the "Mennonite fire marshal"

— Chapter 15 —

Both Plans Grow

Fire and Storm Moves to Salunga Office

No sooner did Mennonite Mutual Aid medical and hospitalization plans move out of the office in 1975 than in 1976 the Fire and Storm Plan moved into the trailer at Salunga. At least it got its nose under the tent. Vernon Charles kept a valuable and complete office at his home. And the local committees still did much of the work at their homes.

The office still carried the Mennonite Brotherly Aid title, and in its reporting to Conference, Mennonite Brotherly Aid meant all the Mennonite Mutual Aid components that the office staff could service—from walk-ins to telephone or letter. But the future of Mennonite Mutual Aid medical lay with the new office on Greenfield Road. By 1980, John Shenk would report that work related to Mennonite Mutual Aid medical "has dropped to a quite low level," involving persons at his congregation and a few other people close to the office. This, he noted in his Mennonite Brotherly Aid quarterly report, was "according to plans." Now Brotherly Aid meant only the Fire and Storm Plan and the motor vehicle Plans.

As the United States was celebrating its bicentennial, the first Plan, Fire and Storm, was basking in its first quarter of a century completed. The wear and tear of those 25 years seemed to make it more hale than in its first tentative juvenile days.

As the events of 1976 evolved, making no-fault an established fact, a staff camaraderie developed in the aluminum trailer that housed the Brotherly Aid offices. Lou Ann Snyder worked full-time for the Brotherly Aid Liability Plan. Donna Nissley worked full-time with Mennonite Automobile Aid collision/comprehensive and MMA's medical plans, which were processed at the Salunga office.

Joan Kreider, the first office employee for the Fire and Storm Plan, worked half-time for that Plan and half-time for the Brotherly Aid Liability Plan. And John Shenk, working one day a week as pastor at East Petersburg, divided his four days 60 to 40 percent, with the Brotherly Aid Liability Plan getting the larger share and Mennonite Mutual Aid programs getting the rest. The foursome gave their combined time this way:

Brotherly Aid Liability Plan	2.1 FTE
Mennonite Mutual Aid	1.4 FTE
Fire and Storm	0.5 FTE

David Miron, the first administrative staff person after John Shenk, is pictured here leading a Liability Plan seminar at a Sharing Programs annual meeting.

Of course, besides the four staff persons in the office, Ivan and Vernon were each working as much as quarter-time at home. In fact, all seven members of the administrative committees, besides John Shenk, received hourly wages for their work.

New Staff Engaged by Fire and Storm

In 1973, Vernon Charles started his staff work from his farmhouse at $3.50 an hour and at nine cents per mile. Before joining the Fire and Storm Plan general committee as treasurer, he had been on the Landisville district local Fire and Storm committee, replacing Edison Gingrich.

Vernon became a kind of Mennonite fire marshal in his new staff-like role. With devotion and style, he kept his car fueled and ready to go anytime a call came, day or night. Although he usually accepted the verdict of the local fire marshal, he still had to come to his own conclusions about the circumstances surrounding a fire or storm loss. As treasurer of the Fire and Storm Plan it was his duty to keep the funds invested. When he started, $125,000 was in the treasury. The original chair, Clarence Harnish, had the impression that nonprofits could not earn interest or they would fall under state control. But Vernon, having been auditor of the East Petersburg Mennonite Church cemetery accounts, knew different.

By the end of his tenure, Vernon was managing $7 million of invested funds. Through the 1970s and 1980s he used certificates of deposit (CDs), which were easy, safe, and good earners. He staggered their terms of maturity so that every month one matured. He always showed up at the bank on the day a cash deposit matured. Once when a cash deposit came due on a Saturday at Brownstown, he went in on Monday. To his chagrin he found out that because the bank had been open Saturday morning he broke his perfect record. For two decades, Vernon was known as a good customer at all but four of the banks having offices in Lancaster County and at other banks in Lebanon and York Counties.

New Staff and Computer Brains

In 1976, Menno Eby, Jr., followed Monroe Garber on the board. Menno, born in 1927, had been on the local Paradise district Fire and Storm committee with Melvin Groff and Paul Andes for some years. The bicentennial year, 1976, left its mark also as the year Brotherly Aid Liability Plan members were involved in six fatal accidents. It was also the year that several groups in Maine, Illinois, Minnesota, and Ohio requested membership in the Brotherly Aid Liability Plan.

Ironically it was also the year that the Brotherly Aid Liability Plan discontinued registration of vehicles not registered in Pennsylvania. This watershed year was also the year a small computer was used for the first time for producing assessments. The bookkeeping was transferred to the computer which Eastern Mennonite Board of Missions used for its work.

In 1977, David Miron began to work three days a week as membership supervisor, relieving John of the membership side of his work. David was married to Jane Wert, the daughter of Earl Wert, one of the ministers who attended the 1954 open meeting at the Mellinger Mennonite Church to explore the possibility of forming an auto liability plan. In 1976, David was ordained as assistant pastor of Blossom Hill Mennonite Church (formerly North End), and from 1978 to 1981, he was the lead pastor.

David's hiring was prompted by a surge in enrollments. The Plan had placed a moratorium on enrolling new members in the years before the enactment of the no-fault law. After the dust settled and the self-insurance agreement with the Department of Transportation was in place, new members were again enrolled. Characteristically, no publicity accompanied the news of the new status of the Liability Plan. Current members spread the word. Growth was slow at first, but soon became a flood. The Plan posted a growth of 20 percent for the 1976-1977 fiscal year. A year later the Liability Plan had "the largest growth in the 23 years of the plan," the annual report stated. The growth was 28 percent! By 1977, the Brotherly Aid Liability Plan had 45 representatives. The office staff could visit only 15 of them that year.

Other changes were coming for the Plan and the Brotherly Aid board. Urban Mennonites were flocking to the Plan, including church members from a variety of ethnic groups. In 1977, Rafael Ramos, pastor of the New

Holland Spanish Mennonite Church, began serving two Spanish-speaking congregations in Lancaster County as a representative for the Liability Plan. A year later, Rafael began a three-year term as a Brotherly Aid board member. During his term, Rafael became involved with the recently formed Spanish Mennonite Council.

But even with David on the staff ready to help handle the great surge in membership, a proportionate increase in claims would surely follow. The office staff in the 10 ft. X 60 ft. trailer sent out a signal that something had to be done to handle the growth and the increasing claims work. In 1977, the vehicles enrolled passed the 7,000 mark. The trailer practically bulged with the flood of over 9,000 enrolled vehicles at the end of 1978.

In January 1978, with David Miron on a nine-month study leave, LaMar Stauffer joined the staff. His first, but part-time responsibility, was secretary of the Fire and Storm Plan, replacing Melvin Graybill who had died several months before. In addition, LaMar assisted John with managing the office and other Liability Plan work as needed. His presence along with David Miron gave John an opportunity to take a much-deserved break. During the summer of 1978 John packed up his family (three children) in a Winnebago purchased for the trip and traveled west for seven weeks. The trip included Mennonite World Conference in Wichita, Kansas.

In September 1979, David Boyd was hired to take over the claims work. Now with staff to supervise membership and claims, a new era began for John. He began to focus on broader issues of Brotherly Aid. He would be well positioned to respond to the changes in the organization a decade later.

In 1975, state law had created a crisis for the Brotherly Aid Liability Plan. Now the well-being of the Liability Plan was being tested by its own weight. Could it handle the phenomenal growth that was almost triple the growth rate allowed for insurance companies? Would another moratorium on new members do enough to make things manageable? Should more staff and larger facilities be explored?

Brotherly Aid Outgrows Trailer

Perhaps it would do both.

On October 1, 1978, the "year of the moratorium" on new members began. Five months later, on February 24, 1979, many of the people closely associated with the Brotherly Aid Liability Plan gathered at Harvest Drive Motel, close to Intercourse, Pennsylvania, for one of several meetings to search the soul of the Liability Plan. That year the conference made an epochal move, retiring after a century the Rules and Discipline, giving more authority to pastors and congregations and moving to full membership status with the denomination.

David H. Boyd
Administrator of the Brotherly Aid Liability Plan

Would that transfer of authority to congregations affect Brotherly Aid? At the same time, the conference reorganized its boards and institutions. Under the new plan most conference work related to the conference through one of four boards: Mission, Congregational Resources, Brotherhood Ministries, or Education.

Brotherly Aid was assigned to the Board of Brotherhood Ministries. After 1979, Brotherly Aid board members would be elected by the conference assembly: all of the ordained persons of Lancaster Conference, including the bishops. The board itself, then, could co-opt four other persons, accommodating the interests of the other church groups associated with the Plan and finding persons with specialized skills who might not otherwise be chosen.

The soul-searching at Harvest Drive included the somber news that a few church persons were sometimes getting lawyers to protect their interests, even in the Brotherly Aid Liability Plan. If the growth after the no-fault law came was attributable to cheaper rates with the Brotherly Aid Liability Plan, was the Plan only a cheaper way to do business or really a unique expression of religious belief? Did the church still have a faith, a practice, a mutual aid to protect? The people at the meeting believed that faith was the driving principle of the Plans.

Rather than retreat, they decided to move the office to larger quarters, increase the staff as needed, and maintain the moratorium until September 30, 1979. The organizational structure should catch up with the growth, they agreed.

The Brotherly Aid office moved to 64 Main Street, into a house rented from the mission board and converted for use as office space. Eight staff

Brotherly Aid Office in the 1980s located at 64 Main Street, Salunga

persons moved into the "new" building: John Shenk, Liability Plan secretary and (unofficially) Brotherly Aid office administrator; David Miron, membership supervisor; Bonnie Bergey, membership assistant; Ruth Harnish, replacing Jeanette Sangrey in the newly created position of Liability Plan assessment handler; David Boyd, claims supervisor; Grace Garber, claims secretary; Lois Pierce, replacing Joan Kreider as Fire and Storm office secretary; and LaMar Stauffer, part-time Fire and Storm secretary. (From 1977 through 1993 LaMar was away on occasion with the Christian Medical Society directing medical missions projects in Central America.)

By 1980, the beginning of the second quarter century of service to the church, Brotherly Aid had eight staff persons. The Liability Plan had 47 volunteer representatives (most of whom also represented MAA). The staff who came on duty in 1980 included: Linda Brubaker, Cathy Mellinger, and Evie Witmer. In 1983, Sharon Brubaker (Horning) and Thelma (Hoover) Stoltzfus joined the staff. By 1985, the staff would increase to 12 with the addition of Jodi (Brubaker) Garber and Dale Ressler. The number of representatives would grow to 57.

The soul-searching and office growth that began at Harvest Drive continued in 1980—the year Ronald Reagan was elected to the presidency of the U.S. At a meeting on May 3 at East Petersburg where John Shenk was pastor, 60 persons, including board members and representatives, pondered such questions as: Are the current risks too large for us to continue as a church-related organization? Does Lancaster Conference or any of the other church bodies participating in Brotherly Aid bear any legal liability?

The costs of claims rose sharply again that year.

In 1981, Mary Herr, Ann Shiner, and Jane Hartzler joined the staff. The assessment base, which had already jumped from $72 to $81, jumped again to $96 per year. Then assessments went to a half-year plan. Airbags were still unknown. Seat belts were standard fare now, but slogans instead of laws were reminding riders to fasten them.

Education For Safety Attempted

In 1981 and for the next year and a half, the Brotherly Aid Liability Plan staff participated in a project to develop study materials called "The Christian on the Highway." At the initiation of Goodville, Brotherly Aid and Mennonite Automobile Aid joined Goodville to produce material for Christians that would supplement the National Safety Council's defensive driving course. It was during a conference at Messiah College that Paul M. Lederach first shared his idea of developing such material. "After all," he argued, "the National Safety Council's defensive driving course already has good Anabaptist peace theology built into it."

Despite Mennonite Automobile Aid's hiring of a staff person to present the course and material in churches and attempts by Goodville and Brotherly Aid to train teachers to use the material, the hope of getting wide use of the materials in the church did not materialize.

Sharing Programs Staff, spring 1995
Seated, left to right: Jane Hartzler, Kim Calabrese, Linda Livengood, John Shenk,
Gretchen Rhodes, Mary Herr, Ruth Clark
Second row: Glen Roth, Judy Petersheim, Lois Pierce, Evelyn Witmer, Helen Miller,
Barbara Stoltzfus, Gina Yoder, Sue Rush, Joan Maxey, Peggy High
Third row: Glenn Steffen, Shawn Nussbaum, David Boyd, David Kammerer, Glen Hess,
Cathy Mellinger, Rhonda Sauder, David Miron, LaMar Stauffer, Dale Ressler
Insert: Wesley Lapp

— Chapter 16 —

More Visions and Issues as Half Century Looms

The 1980s began with nine staff persons. By 1995, the number would be 30.

The Fire and Storm Plan was becoming a friendly "banker brother" to many congregations and church institutions. For example, in 1980 it loaned many thousands of dollars to the Brotherly Aid Liability Plan to meet Pennsylvania's requirement of $1 million security deposit in order to function as a self-insured group. The Plan also loaned $300,000 to the Mennonite Publishing House for construction of a warehouse. Christian Light Publications, Faith Mennonite High School, and Menno Housing borrowed also. Congregations from several participating church bodies were able to build with loans from the Fire and Storm Plan. These funds were available on a somewhat tentative basis because the Fire and Storm Plan needed to maintain sufficient funds in the event of unusual emergencies, such as several fires or severe wind storms in any given year.

The Brotherly Aid Liability Plan began the year 1980 with 6,159 members. By 1995, 29,000 operators participated in the Plan—significantly more than the number of members of Lancaster Mennonite Conference, the founding church body of Brotherly Aid. In 1995, one-third of the Brotherly Aid Liability Plan members came from the founding body. One-fifth came from its sister body, Franconia Conference, and one-tenth from Atlantic Coast Conference. Brethren in Christ and General Conference Mennonites each accounted for eight percent, and Old Order Mennonites for five percent.

Plans Incorporate

In the early part of the 1980s, Lancaster Conference leadership became concerned about the possibility of lawsuits reaching back to the church at large from the activities of the church institutions. With this liability exposure in mind, the conference asked the Brotherly Aid Plans to consider incorporating. Incorporation would raise a legal barrier to liability.

Fire and Storm Administrative Committee, 1995 (L-R): Melvin Groff; LaMar Stauffer, secretary and administrator of Fire and Storm Plan; Sue Rush, staff representative; and Alvin Weaver, chair.

Although the question of incorporation was discussed off and on for several years, it took a change in the federal tax law to bring it about. In 1986, federal tax law changes made the work of the Plans taxable. And, since the income of the Plans represented a "significant" portion of the income of the parent organization (Lancaster Conference), the new tax status of the Plans placed the Conference in jeopardy of losing its tax exempt status. The Brotherly Aid Board agreed to incorporate.

Incorporation Brings Opportunity

The process to incorporate could have been a step away from the roots for Brotherly Aid. Instead, it became an opportunity to more firmly establish roots and more clearly articulate the vision of caring and sharing. One of the first questions asked was, "Under what name shall the Plans incorporate?" Should it be the "Brotherly Aid Board, Incorporated?" That question prompted a discussion of the meaning of names and the long-range vision for Brotherly Aid. In the end, the board and staff chose Sharing Programs of the Lancaster Mennonite Conference, Incorporated. Moving away from the "historic" name, Brotherly Aid, was an attempt to "modernize" on one hand and to expand on the other. In choosing "Sharing Programs," the board and staff expressed a concern that the organization be poised for responding to the needs of church members beyond what the Plans were already doing.

This Sharing Programs meeting with the Vietnamese Mennonite Church occurred to clarify the nature of Sharing Programs. (L): David Miron; (third from L): Dale Ressler; and (far R): Donald Sensenig, interpreter.

Drafting a Mission Statement

Another question raised by incorporation was, "Shouldn't the new corporation have a mission statement?" The legal documents required a statement of purpose for the corporation. Glen Roth, on one of his first assignments, helped to develop and implement a process for writing a mission statement. Staff members, board members, former board members, representatives, and members at large were interviewed. Glen asked each person, "Why Brotherly Aid?" The answers included 34 key words or phrases such as: helping ministry, compassion, ways of caring, openness, saving/investment, servant, leader. Then, on February 18, 1988, at the Landisville Mennonite Church, a first of a kind meeting was held. All the board and staff members met together. The agenda was to take the list of key words and phrases and identify the ten that seemed most significant for the work of Brotherly Aid. Two significant results came from this meeting: a mission statement that continues to guide Sharing Programs in its work and development and a sense that the new corporation would be an umbrella for caring and sharing activities.

MISSION STATEMENT

It shall be the mission of Sharing Programs of the Lancaster Mennonite Conference to assist the Mennonite family of churches in caring, sharing and burden-bearing. All activities and programs shall be planned with the goals of exemplifying Christ and fostering spiritual sensitivity to God and to one another.

It is the intention of Sharing Programs in carrying out its mission to:

- *Maintain a sensitivity to God's presence in all planning and programming.*

- *Relate to all persons in the spirit of compassion and justice, fairness and impartiality.*

- *Base all decisions on the principles of honesty and trust.*

- *Maintain a high level of personal and organizational accountability and integrity.*

- *Exercise and encourage careful stewardship in meeting human need.*

- *Design programs that meet identified need among the members.*

- *Help the church equip its members for a ministry of caring and sharing.*

- *Respond sensitively and creatively to changes within the church and in society.*

A New Way of Accounting

The new tax laws had another impact on the Brotherly Aid Plans. The plans had to change the way they did their accounting. For 37 years (32 for the Liability Plan), the plans counted the money collected and the money spent each year. If the money collected did not equal the money spent, then the members could be depended upon to pay more. Only four times in all those years did the plans ask for more from the members.

The new tax law treated the plans like insurance companies. Insurance companies use a different way of counting: the accrual method. And insurance companies are allowed to show the claims waiting for settlement as "money spent." So, for the first time, an accounting firm was hired to review the books and help set up the new accounting procedures.

Impact of the Culture

The secular forces affecting individuals and congregations in the decade of the 1980s affected Brotherly Aid members, too. For example, 20 participants in the Brotherly Aid Liability Plan had to be dropped in 1986 because of alcohol or drug use. The high cost of medical costs kept spiraling upward. In 1987, two accidents required claim payments to the maximum of $300,000.

Growth Forces Questions

The Brotherly Aid Liability Plan's growth staggered the imagination through the 1980s until it peaked in 1991 when it could boast 30,356 agreements. Assessments from those agreements that year amounted to over $8 million. A little less than one-sixteenth of that went into paying the staff who managed the burden sharing through this Plan. Under the accrual method of accounting, the Plan held more funds for paying pending claims which increased assessments but made assessments more predictable for the members. This change was a shift from the original thinking of those who founded the Plan and raised the question for some, "Are we having less faith now that we need to have the money right away?"

As the assessments increased to match the cost of accidents as they happened, the assessment dollars started to cross a line for some of the members in the plan. That line was the cost of regular insurance which for some members would be less than the assessment of the Brotherly Aid Liability Plan. The members who lived in the parts of Pennsylvania where that was the case asked why. In 1991, this led the plan to assessing differently based on geographic areas and operator history. Even after the geographic rates went into effect, the areas with highest rates paid much less than the commercial insurance costs while the lowest rate areas were closer to the insurance rates. As of this writing, members in Philadelphia had their rates subsidized from $20 to $163 per agreement.

In a sense, Fire and Storm had always been rating by geography because the value of a building floated with its location, and assessments were made per thousand dollars of valuation. Fire and Storm offered a discount for timely payments in a year with no claims filed.

Educating for Stewardship

While the Brotherly Aid Liability Plan assumed that members were bound to each other to share liabilities, people were beginning to wonder if they should not also be accountable for careless driving that causes collisions. In a ten-month period in 1984-85, David Boyd, head of the claims department, noted that $2,148,000 was paid for collisions for which Brotherly Aid Liability Plan members were partially or wholly responsible. During the same period, only $414,900 was paid where a Brotherly Aid Liability Plan member did not cause the accident.

"What I would really like to see," he is quoted in an article in the November 1985 *Missionary Messenger*, "is a plan by which church members would be more accountable to each other for their driving habits. Mutual accountability would help people realize that one's driving habits affect others, not just in mutual aid costs, but in saving of lives and preventing of emotional and physical suffering."

It was no wonder he was concerned. In 1985, the Brotherly Aid Liability Plan added 2,000 vehicles, its largest annual growth. The equivalent of four and a half claims were reported each working day, and one accident that year cost $800,000, the largest in the history of the Plan. That same year David Boyd and Cathy Mellinger received their appraiser's licenses and Dale Ressler joined the team, working with claims. The addition of an 800 telephone line made contacting the office easier.

The Fire and Storm Plan renewed its efforts at stewardship of property by urging the installation of smoke detectors and other measures to protect property.

The 64 Main Street office was bursting with activity; by 1987, Brotherly Aid occupied the first floor of the house next door, 60 Main Street. But no sooner was the second house occupied than in 1988, a new possibility was uttered in reports to the board—moving into church-owned property beside Lancaster Mennonite High School. By now 16 staff persons were in the two houses, the 1987 recruits being Janice Burkhart, Glen Hess, Glen Roth, Rhonda Sauder, and Denise Witmer.

Sharing Programs office, along with other offices and businesses, was located at 2160 Lincoln Highway East, Lancaster, Pennsylvania.

Move to 2160

On August 24, 1989, every file, computer disk, and pencil was moved to 2160 Lincoln Highway East, Lancaster, Pennsylvania, to a second-floor space purchased in a condominium agreement. For the first time, Sharing Programs owned the floor it sat its desks on. It bought an Alpha Micro 4000 multi-user computer system that currently has 35 terminals and 10 printers.

In 1989, as the 40th anniversary for the Fire and Storm Plan and the 35th anniversary of the Liability Plan approached, even amid all the changes of recent years, it was clear that the basic interaction of each Plan had not changed. Stopping in at the Buckwalters in Smoketown, for example, to register a change in cars was very much the same as it was 30 years ago. And so was the wording on the agreement.

Familiar Faces Begin to Leave

New faces coming to Sharing Programs meant familiar faces were departing. In 1993, Nancy Stauffer became the first woman Board member.

David and Marian Buckwalter, BALP representatives. David was appointed assistant treasurer in 1958. Marian and David continue to serve as BALP representatives from their home in Smoketown.

However, also in 1993, only four years after the move to 2160 Lincoln Highway, two persons whose names were practically synonymous with Brotherly Aid retired. Ivan Leaman, the first treasurer of the Brotherly Aid Liability Plan at its first meeting at Kendig Miller's house in 1955, continued in that position until he retired in 1993 at age 87. His career with the Liability Plan followed it through the Miller house, the Shenk house, the office in the mission headquarters building, the trailer beside the mission building in Salunga, the Main Street house in Salunga and, finally, to 2160. That same year, Vernon Charles completed his 24th year as treasurer of Fire and Storm and retired. In addition, he served as field man from 1973 to 1993.

Neither Ivan's nor Vernon's positions were continued with the exact same job description. Ivan's work was transferred to the accounting department. Vernon's work was shared by the accounting department and by LaMar Stauffer in the central office.

On January 19, 1995, John Harnish, who wrote his very first agreement in 1955 (the first year of the Plan), retired as representative. Also on September 20, 1995, Melvin L. Groff retired as a member of the Fire and Storm

Plan administrative committee, having served in this position for 21 years. He was well prepared for this work, having served for several years as a Fire and Storm local committeeman before his appointment to the administrative committee.

With the retirement of Andrew Shaub in 1990 came the end to the presence of the original members on the Board.

John and Myrtle Shenk (1995). The Shenks lived here for three months in 1959 at the former home of Myrtle's parents, Jacob and Katie Brenneman, following their term of voluntary service in Homestead, Florida. This was where John was invited to join the Brotherly Aid team.

John B. Shenk Retires

The year 1995 brought a close to the Sharing Programs work of not only Melvin Groff and John Harnish, but "Mr. Brotherly Aid" himself, John B. Shenk. John's work with the plans had begun when full-time work for a church agency was an exception to the rule. Actually, John tells people that he technically never worked full time for Sharing Programs. He went from voluntary service with the mission board in Florida to the Earl King construction crew to the Weaver Bookstore to tent-making pastoring at East Petersburg Mennonite Church. Throughout his tenure with Brotherly Aid/ Sharing Progams, he drew a part-time salary supplemented by income from East Petersburg Mennonite Church.

On June 30, 1994, John sent a letter to Andrew Miller, the chair of the Sharing Programs Board of directors. "I believe," wrote John, "that the time has come for some change at Sharing Programs. It is very close to 35 years

President J. Glen Hostetler and the Sharing Programs Board, 1995.

(L-R): Lynn R. Zimmerman, James H. Thomas, Clayton R. Nissley, Alvin M. Weaver (vice-chair), Nelson C. Hoover (secretary), J. Glen Hostetler (president of Sharing Programs), Nelson W. Martin (treasurer), John M. Weaver, David H. Zimmerman, Andrew G. Miller (chair), Kenneth D. Roberts, and Nancy L. Stauffer.

ago that I began helping Kendig Miller as secretary of the fledgling Liability Plan. It will be 35 years on January 1, 1995, since I began serving the plan as secretary. We both know there has been much growth and many changes during these years."

The letter, which he would read to the entire staff a few days later, continued: "I am making plans for retirement about June 30, 1995. If the Lord wills, I will be 65 on June 5 of next year. This will leave about one year for the board to find my replacement and have this person ready to take charge upon my leaving. To you and the rest of the board I owe a debt of gratitude for your generous support over the years. The same is true of the staff. May the Lord grant wisdom in finding my successor. May the best years for Brotherly Aid/Sharing Programs still be in the future."

The board named a search committee and found the successor to John in the board's treasurer, J. Glen Hostetler. Glen, after graduating from Elizabethtown College, first worked as a certified public accountant before being ordained as a deacon at the Mount Joy Mennonite Church. He later accepted administrative posts with the Lancaster Mennonite Conference Office and Mennonite Economic Development Associates.

Upon taking office July 1, 1995, Glen wrote to the members of the Plans in Sharing Program's newsletter, *Journey,* "John's quiet demeanor and steady leadership style have earned him the admiration and respect of everyone associated with the Brotherly Aid Plans. During his watch, the plans grew and developed into the network of support and mutual aid that blesses so many each year."

"It is my pleasure to greet you as the newly appointed president of Sharing Programs (the title of the office previously was general administrator). I owe a special debt of gratitude to John for his patience and graciousness during our transition period. John went beyond the second mile to provide a good orientation, and I thank him for it."

In 1990s, Search For Authentic Mutuality Continues

Like any organized activity, Sharing Programs, Inc., has to consider whether it is still fresh with conviction of Christian mutual aid or whether it is becoming an agency protecting its turf. As the 1990s moved toward a new century, the Plans kept grappling with the same forces they had in 1950 and 1955: fairness with a Christian perspective. Is the $300,000 limit for auto liability fair? Should Fire and Storm extend coverage to liability on property?

In Glen Hostetler's words: "Future programs are shaped by new views and preferences. Existing priorities are called into question and placed on the table for reevaluation. As the plans grow and develop, current forms may need to yield to newer ones in order to maintain a satisfactory level of service."

Fifth and sixth graders at South Christian Street Mennonite Church participate in the Sharing Program drawing contest to illustrate ways of caring for one another in time of need.

"You have our commitment," Glen wrote in his first message to the over 30,000 members of the Plans, "to retain the essential elements of mutual aid while upgrading the programs to meet your needs."

Even while the Plans had veterans serving them for four decades, the board had already been asking whether the next generation is catching the mutual aid spirit. Glen Roth took the mutual aid vision of caring for each other to children. In 1987, Sharing Programs sponsored an essay contest in which more than 600 children participated. In 1988, students in 16 Mennonite elementary and high schools participated in a "contest" to design visuals of mutual aid. In 1993, Good Books published *Shared Burdens*, a book edited by Glen Roth and Sue Schlabach.

When Glen Hostetler succeeded John, discussions with other mutual aid organizations were already under way to find ways to provide comprehensive services to members. In particular, at the time of this writing, Sharing Programs was one of twelve mutual aid organizations involved in cooperative endeavors in the future. Glen wrote in the October 1995 *Journey* that "there are several significant challenges ahead, and I invite you to walk with us as we proceed. As a result of our participation in a cooperative effort among auto and property aid associations across the country, we expect to be able to offer some expanded services soon. If all goes well, by next spring we will

Christy Shull, Grand Prize Winner for Logo Contest, is congratulated by Andrew Miller, Sharing Programs board chairman. Christy was in grade 11 at Lancaster Mennonite High School, December 1989.

be able to offer our own collision and comprehensive coverage to members of the Liability Plan. In addition, work continues toward making personal liability coverage available to complement the property physical damage provisions of the Fire and Storm Plan."

The mission statement of the plans spells out that Sharing Programs shall "assist the Mennonite family of churches in caring, sharing and burden-bearing." All of this, the statement makes clear, shall be done "with the goal of exemplifying Christ and fostering spiritual sensitivity to God and to one another."

The tiny acorn planted by the people at Byerland, watered at Vine Street, blessed by the persons gathered at Indiantown, was now a secure oak, with boughs protecting a large cluster of churches and Christians who believe in sharing their burdens and joys.

Annual Meeting, December 3, 1993, at
Lancaster Mennonite High School.

Postscript

by Glenn M. Lehman

For the months that Sharing Programs provided desk space in the home office for me to write this history, I rubbed shoulders with honest, hard-working servants of Christ in a church institution. At the first weekly staff meeting of my sojourn, I noticed how testimony and prayer were a part of the agenda. That surprised even me, a veteran of many staff meetings in other church and congregational settings. Here where calculators and computers buzz at the speed of light and high-tech machines figure out what fair share of your burden is mine to pay, prayer has a higher agenda status than I assumed it would.

After this extraordinary opportunity to see Acts 2 close up, 20th-century style, I am not surprised at the devotions and prayer.

These sharing plans had a vision that drew people together who were otherwise quite different. The mutual aid vision had an uncanny ability to draw together in a common cause the progressive and the cautious, the ordained and the lay, the new churches and the old. The early church air that these plans breathe is favorable to church groups uniting in a common cause. The plans support the cause of peace, because conflict, hate, and war destroy exactly what the plans protect. The plans support good stewardship of the resources of the earth, especially the lives of individuals created in the image of God. Safe driving, fire protection, and resources for medical care (1965-75) are good both for the plans and for the whole of God's creation. Death, accident, and destruction are not good for the plans nor for the participants.

Close to the end of this writing I attended a staff meeting and heard John Shenk read the letter of retirement he sent to the board. Andrew Miller, chairman of the board, seated beside him, explained how the purpose of the plans would not change even though John would retire.

A few staff meetings later, John announced to the staff that his turnip crop had been pretty good that year and that he had several dozen to give away. I thought of Stoner Krady's vegetables sold in Lancaster. When Stoner retired from the Sponsoring Committee, the plans continued and increased nonetheless. The plans could not prosper without dedicated and able staff. But the vision transcends any one person, even the chief staff person in the office.

Yet the real work of Sharing Programs happens outside office walls. I was writing this history when the East District church lost its building. Without the network of dollars within the Fire and Storm Plan, the East District Mennonite Church would have struggled long and hard to recoup the devastating loss of $400,000 by arson. At the dedication of the new building, East District gave a ringing testimony of the power of God in the church. Several newspapers, radio, and television stations carried the good news of love in Christ overcoming evil and crossing boundaries of time and place.

Between the Hess haircuts in 1948 and the $14 million in losses spread among church members in 1994, what has Sharing Programs achieved?

Did it produce heroes? No, just quiet ordinary believers who do not clamor for fame and who do not shrink from duty. At critical moments people of renown in other aspects of church life, from Stoner Krady to James Hess to Clarence Lutz to Paul Landis to many others, have stepped in from their otherwise established positions of church reputations to tip things right.

Did Brotherly Aid produce mountaintop experiences of faith? No, but many helping hands in many valleys of despair kept many families alive and happy.

Did it change the course of the church? No, but it had a share in keeping alive a central theme of the Pentecostal New Testament church: having goods in common.

Is it the primary institution for teaching and passing the faith to the next generation? No, but through the systems of economic exchange young people see adults confront both the needed lip service to God and the real stewardship of God's created world.

"No" to all of the above questions?

The longer I studied the history and talked to the Sharing Programs people, went to annual meetings, local representative meetings, and read the early documents and interviewed long-time participants, the more those questions took on a dimension I didn't see before.

The selfless faith of signing up in April 1950 all one's worldly property to a plan with no assets other than the good word of the others in the church produces heroes of faith. Heroes? Yes! Mountaintop experiences? Yes!

A will to stretch the church across the necessary but somewhat artificial lines of denomination and conference from the suspicion of the 1950s to the individualism of the 1990s constitutes a form of outreach and risking of the faith. Yes! Brotherly Aid is a story of strong church theology, of devotion to the body of Christ, of people taking risks, not just protecting themselves.

I see a program obedient to its founding church's mandate, yet creating a cautious alliance with the specialized insurance professions, boundaries between the world and the kingdom of God, and flexibility to respond to economic realities as they evolve.

Heroes? Mountaintop experiences and spiritual power? Yes. Found at every need met: "see how they love each other...."

The teaching? Yes. Deeds more than documents.

"Well done, thou good and faithful steward" might be one of its mottoes.

Brotherly Aid Principle

Enhance—

not interfere with—

the life of the congregation.

Appendix

Sharing Programs Board Members

Sharing Programs Board Officers

Sharing Programs Staff Roster, 1965-1995

Brotherly Aid Fire and Storm Plan General Committee/
Administrative Committee

Brotherly Aid Fire and Storm Plan Representatives

Brotherly Aid Liability Plan General Committee/
Administrative Committee

Brotherly Aid Liability Plan Representatives

Annual Meetings

Association of Mennonite Aid Societies

Mennonite Indemnity, Inc.

Sharing Programs Board Members *

1965-1967	Elmer G. Martin
1965-1968	Simon Bucher
1965-1972	Edwin H. Gehman
1965-1989	James H. Hess
1965-1976	Monroe E. Garber
1965-1983	Clair B. Eby
1965-1977; 1978-1990	Andrew H. Shaub
1965-1986	Ivan G. Charles, Jr.
1965-1978	Alvin Sauder
1967-1973	Elmer G. Martin, Jr.
1968-1978	A. David Buckwalter
1972-1993	Paul Z. Musser
1973-1982	Joseph H. Weaver
1976-1982	Menno L. Eby, Jr.
1977-1981	Larry W. Newswanger
1978-1981	Rafael Ramos
1981-	John M. Weaver
1981-	James H. Thomas

---

* From 1965 to November 1987, the Board was known as the Brotherly Aid Board. Effective November 1987 to the present time, it has been the Board of Sharing Programs of the Lancaster Mennonite Conference, Inc.

1982-1982	Willis Burkholder attended only one meeting; killed in a small plane crash
1982-	Andrew G. Miller
1982-1992	Glenn H. Shenk
1982-1983	Isaac W. Gehman
1983-1995	Paul W. Weaver
1983-1988	Harvey M. Zimmerman
1985-	Alvin M. Weaver
1987-1995	J. Glen Hostetler
1989-	Clayton R. Nissley
1989-1992	David S. Hess
1991-	Nelson C. Hoover
1992-1995	Ray W. Beyer
1992-	Kenneth D. Roberts
1993-	Nancy L. Stauffer
1995-	Nelson W. Martin
1995-	David H. Zimmerman
1995-	Lynn R. Zimmerman

Sharing Programs Board Officers *

May 8, 1965

President	Andrew H. Shaub
Vice-President	Clair B. Eby
Secretary	Monroe E. Garber

April 16, 1969

Chairman	Andrew H. Shaub
Vice-Chairman	Clair B. Eby
Secretary	Elmer G. Martin, Jr.

April 27, 1972

Chairman	James H. Hess
Vice-Chairman	Clair B. Eby
Secretary	Paul Z. Musser

April 23, 1981

Chairman	Andrew H. Shaub
Vice-Chairman	Clair B. Eby
Secretary	Paul Z. Musser

---

* From 1965 to November 1987, the board was known as the Brotherly Aid Board. Effective November 1987 to the present, it has been the Board of Sharing Programs of the Lancaster Mennonite Conference, Inc.

April 22, 1982

Chairman	Andrew H. Shaub
Vice-Chairman	Ivan G. Charles, Jr.
Secretary	Paul Z. Musser

April 26, 1984

Chairman	Andrew G. Miller
Vice-Chairman	Glenn H. Shenk
Secretary	Paul Z. Musser

April 25, 1985

Chairman	Andrew G. Miller
Vice-Chairman	John M. Weaver
Secretary	Paul Z. Musser

April 28, 1988

Chairman	Andrew G. Miller
Vice-Chairman	John M. Weaver
Secretary	Paul Z. Musser
Treasurer	J. Glen Hostetler

April 27, 1989

Chairman	Andrew G. Miller
Vice-Chairman	Glenn H. Shenk
Secretary	Paul Z. Musser
Treasurer	J. Glen Hostetler

May 7, 1992

Chairman	Andrew G. Miller
Assistant Chairman	Alvin M. Weaver
Secretary	Paul Z. Musser
Treasurer	J. Glen Hostetler

May 6, 1993

Chairman	Andrew G. Miller
Assistant Chairman	Alvin M. Weaver
Secretary	Nelson C. Hoover
Treasurer	J. Glen Hostetler

May 4, 1995

Chairman	Andrew G. Miller
Assistant Chairman	Alvin M. Weaver
Secretary	Nelson C. Hoover
Treasurer	Nelson W. Martin

Sharing Programs Staff Roster
*1965-1995**

John B. Shenk	- 2/1/1965 - 6/30/1995
M. Elaine Zuck	- 3/29/1965 - 8/27/1965 (part-time)
Ruth Ann Zimmerman (Martin)	- 8/16/1965 - 3/31/1967 (part-time)
Marian E. Buckwalter	- 6/1/1966 - 2/1/1968 (part-time)
Lloyd Zeager	- 6/5/1967 - 9/7/1972
	- 5/28/1974 - 8/30/1974
Barbara A. Keller (Sitkowski)	- 9/15/1969 - 12/31/1975
Eileen N. Gerlach (Hoover)	- 9/5/1972 - 5/4/1973
M. Laverne (Kreider) Oberholtzer	- 5/1/1973 - 4/30/1975
Donna Sue (Nissley) Wenger	- 3/15/1975 - 4/8/1977
Joan E. Kreider (Buckwalter)	- 11/17/1975 - 8/31/1979
Lou Ann Snyder (Gehman)	- 12/15/1975 - 7/21/1978
David Miron	- 1/1/1977 - 9/1/1977
	- 6/5/1978 -
Grace R. Garber	- 4/4/1977 - 7/16/1980
LaMar E. Stauffer	- 1/3/1978 -
Bonnie S. Bergey	- 7/10/1978 - 6/15/1981

---

* From 1965 to November 1987, Sharing Programs was known as Brotherly Aid. In November 1987 the organization was incorporated as Sharing Programs of the Lancaster Mennonite Conference, Inc.

Janette Sangrey (Barber)	-	5/1/1979 - 8/13/1979
A. Lois Pierce	-	8/6/1979 - 12/31/1981
	-	1/9/1991 -
Ruth E. Harnish (Yoder)	-	8/15/1979 - 6/30/1980
David H. Boyd	-	9/24/1979 -
Linda G. (Brubaker) Beiler	-	6/17/1980 - 5/31/1987
Cathy A. Mellinger	-	7/8/1980 -
Evelyn I. Witmer	-	9/3/1980 -
Mary M. Herr	-	6/22/1981 -
Ann E. Shiner	-	11/1/1981 - 8/31/1983
E. Jane Hartzler	-	12/2/1981 -
Sharon E. Brubaker (Horning)	-	8/1/1983 - 10/19/1984
Thelma J. (Hoover) Stoltzfus	-	8/29/1983 - 9/8/1989
Jodi L. (Brubaker) Garber	-	2/11/1985 - 2/29/1988
Dale E. Ressler	-	4/15/1985 -
Lloyd B. Denlinger	-	2/7/1986 - 8/25/1989 (part-time)
Kathy L. (Lippiatt) Noll	-	2/2/1987 - 9/18/1987
Glen E. Hess	-	2/9/1987 -
Denise Y. (Witmer) Hess	-	6/9/1987 - 9/24/1992
Rhonda L. Sauder	-	6/15/1987 - 12/8/1995
Glen A. Roth	-	8/3/1987 -
Janice L. Burkhart	-	9/17/1987 - 3/17/1989
Wesley M. Lapp	-	2/1/1988 -
Joan M. Maxey	-	2/16/1988 - 10/4/1990
	-	5/11/1992 -
Janet B. Hoover	-	10/11/1988 - 11/2/1989 (part-time)
John D. Nafziger	-	11/7/1988 - 6/13/1994
Barbara J. Peters	-	3/9/1989 - 11/2/1990

Andrew H. Shaub	-	8/19/1989 - 5/31/1991 (part-time)
Ruth C. Shaub	-	9/8/1989 - 5/31/1991 (part-time)
B. Sue Rush	-	8/21/1989 -
Brenda M. Landis (Weaver)	-	9/18/1989 - 8/31/1990
Joy M. Hershey	-	11/20/1989 - 11/3/1992
Gina G. (Groff) Yoder	-	6/15/1990 -
J. Mark Zook	-	7/2/1990 - 12/31/1992
Sue V. Schlabach	-	9/12/1990 - 11/30/1992
Lisa M. Metzler	-	9/24/1990 - 10/9/1992
Jean F. Lehman (Blackwell)	-	9/26/1990 - 6/14/1991
Sue E. Lincoln	-	11/9/1990 - 5/14/1992
David M. Kammerer	-	1/7/1991 -
Lynette M. Mellinger (Nisly)	-	5/20/1991 - 10/4/1991 (part-time)
Elizabeth S. Diffenderfer	-	5/31/1991 - (part-time)
Melvin N. Diffenderfer	-	5/31/1991 - (part-time)
Kim M. Calabrese	-	6/3/1991 -
Ella Mae Mellinger	-	7/12/1991 - (part-time)
Judy E. Petersheim (Stauffer)	-	9/8/1992 - 4/14/1995
Barbara J. Stoltzfus	-	9/10/1992 -
Helen L. Miller	-	9/14/1992 -
Peggy High	-	10/12/1992 -
Glenn W. Steffen	-	12/1/1992 -
Gretchen M. (Newman) Rhodes	-	12/28/1992 -
Ruth C. Clark	-	1/18/1993 -
Linda J. Livengood	-	8/23/1993 -
Shawn M. Nussbaum	-	9/13/1993 -
Cynthia A. Kilhefner	-	3/9/1995 -
J. Glen Hostetler	-	5/22/1995 -
Eunice C. Ground	-	11/6/1995 -

Brotherly Aid
Fire and Storm Plan
General Committee/Administrative Committee

Chairman

Clarence H. Harnish	1950-1973
Alvin M. Weaver	1974-present

Secretary

Roy E. Ulrich	1950-1963
Melvin M. Graybill	1963-1977
LaMar E. Stauffer	1978-1993

Secretary/Treasurer

LaMar E. Stauffer	1993-present

Treasurer

Andrew H. Shaub	1950-1959
Raymond S. Sauder	1959-1969
Vernon H. Charles	1969-1993

Fourth Member

Melvin L. Groff	1974-1995
Clayton R. Nissley	1995-present

Field Man

Vernon H. Charles	1973-1993

Brotherly Aid
Fire and Storm Plan
Representatives

The following are persons who have served as Brotherly Aid Fire and Storm Plan representatives in the past or are continuing to serve as representatives with approximate dates when they began serving. Representatives who were active as of November 1995 are marked with an asterisk.

Acevedo, Herminio (Philadelphia City)
Andes, Paul L. (Hershey-Paradise)
Bange, Norman (York-Adams)
Bedford, Bruce (Williamsport/Milton)
Beiler, Aaron S. * (New York - Madison)
Beiler, John H. Jr. (New York - Madison)
Bender, Ralph * N. (Northern Pennsylvania)
Benner, Galen * N. (Landisville)
Beyers, Ray W. * (Hammer Creek)
Beyer, Russel (Hammer Creek)
Bowman, Paul (New Danville)
Breneman, Clifford (Manor)
Brubaker, John (Manor)
Brubaker, Roy (Juniata)
Bucher, Harold (Alabama and NW of Florida)
Bucher, John (Manheim)
Buckwalter, John (New York City)
Buckwalter, Paul N. (Mellinger)
Buckwalter, Robert (Southern New York)
Byler, Daniel (Juniata)
Campbell, John E. * (Groffdale)
Carpenter, Stanley M. * (Landisville)
Charles, Mahlon L. * (Elizabethtown)
Charles, Vernon (Landisville)
Chau, Howard * (Philadelphia City)
Clymer, Martin (Mellinger)

Coin, Roger (Alabama North)
Davis, James * (Juniata)
Diem, Ivan C. (Juniata)
Dietz, John S. * (York)
Ebersole, Marlin (Cumberland)
Eby, Menno L. * (Hershey-Paradise)
Engle, Irvin (Millwood)
Engle, Nicolas (Millwood)
Esbenshade, Adam (New England)
Eshleman, Howard (New Danville)
Fisher, Brian K. & Vicky E. (Delaware Valley, New Jersey)
Forry, Alvan D. * (York-Adams)
Forry, Lloyd (Landisville)
Fox, Daniel (Landisville)
Fox, Edwin S. (Bowmansville/Reading)
Frederick, Isaac (Florida - Tampa, Sarasota, Immokalee)
Frey, Eugene R. * (Lancaster City)
Frey, Rodger A * (York-Adams)
Gehman, Edwin (Martindale/Weaverland)
Gehman, John E. * (Juniata)
Gehman, John H. * (Alabama South - Northwest Florida)
Ginder, Isaac (Juniata)
Gingrich, Edison (Landisville)
Givens, Clarence L. * (Elizabethtown)
Glick, Allen (Juniata)
Gochnauer, Robert, Sr. (Willow Street, Strasburg)
Gockley, Darrell L. * (Bowmansville/Reading)
Good, Charles (Willow Street, Strasburg)
Good, Harlen S. (Hammer Creek)
Good, Harold L. * (South Carolina)
Good, Mahlon (Bowmansville/Reading)
Good, Sanford (Lebanon and Berks Counties)
Graybill, Eli (Juniata)
Greiner, Dale E. * (White Oak Church of the Brethren)
Groff, Hershey L. (Williamsport/Milton)
Groff, John (Landisville)
Groff, Lester W. (Martindale)
Groff, Marvin B. * (Northern Pennsylvania)
Groff, Melvin L. * (Hershey-Paradise)
Groff, Wade (Willow Street, Strasburg)
Haldeman, Harold (Manheim)
Halteman, Ray A. * (Cumberland)
Harnish, C. Donald * (New Danville)

Harnish, J. Nelson * (Mellinger)
Harnish, Robert (Mellinger)
Heimbach, Robert W. & Vicky J. * (Juniata)
Helmuth, Clarence (Florida - Tampa, Sarasota, Immokalee)
Herr, Glenn E. * (York-Adams)
Herr, Harold M. (York-Adams)
Herr, Melvin N. * (Groffdale)
Hershey, Benjamin D. * (Florida - Tampa, Sarasota, Immokalee)
Hershey, Richard (Hess-Landis Valley)
Hess, David S. * (New Danville)
Hess, Henry (New Danville)
Hess, Joseph H. (Cumberland)
Hess, Keith L. * (Alabama South/Northwest Florida)
Hess, H. Laverne * (Northern Pennsylvania)
Hess, Paul (New Danville)
High, Henry (Bowmansville/Reading)
High, John (Illinois)
Horst, Aaron Z. * (Martindale)
Horst, Amos E. * (Florida - Tampa, Sarasota, Immokalee)
Horst, Harold M. * (Groffdale)
Horst, Joseph (Alabama - Northwest of Florida)
Horst, Melvin H. (Chambersburg)
Horst, Roy R. * (Florida - Tampa, Sarasota, Immokalee)
Horst, Vernon D. * (Chambersburg)
Hostetter, Harvey M. (Manor)
Hostetter, Isaac E. * (Willow Street, Strasburg)
Hostetter, Virgil (Washington/Baltimore)
Huber, John D. (Alabama South - Northwest Florida)
Hurst, Willie (Southern New York)
Hyland, Dorothy A. * (Northeastern Pennsylvania)
Kauffman, Ammon (Millwood)
Kauffman, Melvin (Northern Pennsylvania)
Keefer, Earl E., Sr. * (Free Grace Brethren in Christ)
Keener, Gerry H. * (New York City)
Keens, R. Samuel * (Hess-Landis Valley)
Kennel, John (Millwood)
Khuu, Peter * (Philadelphia City)
King, David M. * (Millwood)
King, Isaac S. (Millwood)
King, Naaman (Millwood)
Klassen, Ervin J. * (Alabama North)
Kolb, Marvin A. (Florida - Tampa, Sarasota, Immokalee)
Krantz, Paul (Willow Street, Strasburg)

Kratzer, Harold (Juniata)
Kraybill, Wilmer G. * (Morgantown)
Kreider, John (Willow Street, Strasburg)
Kreider, Lloyd H. * (New Danville; Willow Street, Strasburg)
Kulp, Samuel (Weaverland)
Kurtz, Richard K. & Cindy (Williamsport/Milton)
Landis, Elvin N. * (Hess-Landis Valley)
Landis, John H. * (Northern Pennsylvania)
Landis, Paul R. * (Williamsport/Milton)
Landis, Richard (Mellinger)
Lantz, James (Mellinger)
Leaman, Ben (Mellinger)
Leaman, Benjamin D., Jr. (Mellinger)
Lefever, Abram T. * (Lebanon and Berks Counties)
Lehman, Jesse W. * (Lebanon and Berks Counties)
Lehman, Mahlon L. * (Elizabethtown)
Longenecker, Phares (Elizabethtown)
Martin, Amos (Lebanon and Berks Counties)
Martin, David (Mellinger)
Martin, Elmer (Lebanon and Berks Counties)
Martin, Emanuel (Lebanon and Berks Counties)
Martin, Ezra M. (Hammer Creek)
Martin, Joseph B. * (Manheim)
Martin, Kenneth (Martindale/Weaverland)
Martin, Larry L. * (Bowmansville/Reading)
Martin, Lester E. * (Chambersburg)
Martin, Marvin Z. * (Bowmansville/Reading)
Martin, Paul (Martindale/Weaverland)
Martinez, Vincent (New York City)
Mast, Oliver (Morgantown)
Meck, Jay A. (Hershey-Paradise)
Metzler, John (Manheim)
Miller, Alvin B. * (Southern New York)
Miller, Claude (New Danville)
Miller, P. Raymond (Landisville)
Miller, J. Robert (Williamsport/Milton)
Miller, Uriah J. * (Bedford - Oakland, Maryland)
Mohler, Galen (Bowmansville/Reading)
Moody, Ricky * (Alabama North)
Musser, Carl Z. * (Hammer Creek)
Musser, Paul Z. (Hammer Creek)
Musser, J. Robert * (Willow Street, Strasburg)
Myer, Elias (Mellinger)

Myers, Reuben D. * (Williamsport/Milton)
Nauman, Jacob (Manheim)
Ness, Reuben J. (York-Adams)
Neuenschwander, Robert D. (Southern New York)
Newcomer, Earl L. * (Manor)
Nissley, Clayton R. * (Manheim)
Nissley, John (Manheim)
Nissley, Lloyd E. (Elizabethtown)
Noll, C. Robert * (Manor)
Nolt, Ronald (New York City)
Peachy, John (Washington/Baltimore)
Peifer, Clarence (Washington/Baltimore)
Pfautz, Leroy R. (Groffdale)
Prior, Cathy (Williamsport/Milton)
Ranck, Elvin (Mellinger)
Ranck, Merle L. *(Millwood)
Ranck, R. Glenn (Philadelphia City)
Reitz, H. Weaver (New Danville)
Risser, Christ (Manheim)
Rohrer, Elmer H. * (Manor)
Sanchez, Carlos (Philadelphia City)
Sauder, Alvin (Martindale/Weaverland)
Sauder, Joseph P. * (Washington/Baltimore)
Sauder, Raymond (Groffdale)
Schnupp, Leon G. * (Delaware Valley, South)
Serrano, Mario * (Philadelphia City)
Shank, Melvin (York-Adams)
Shank, Paul (Chambersburg)
Sharp, Crist (Juniata)
Shaub, Andrew H. (Manor)
Shearer, Harold (Florida - Tampa, Sarasota, Immokalee)
Sheeler, James G. (Cumberland)
Shellenberger, Shelly (Landisville)
Shelly, Eugene (New York City)
Shelly, Paul (Alabama and Northwest of Florida)
Shenk, Glenn (New Danville)
Shertzer, Charles (Manor)
Showalter, Paul D. * (Chambersburg)
Siegrist, Landis (Mellinger)
Smith, Peter G. (Elizabethtown)
Smoker, Elmer (Millwood)
Smoker, Irvin (Northern Pennsylvania)
Smoker, Omer S. * (Millwood)

Stauffer, Charles (Bowmansville/Reading)
Steffy, Noah (Groffdale)
Stoltzfus, J. Parke * (Juniata)
Stoner, Titus B. * (Landisville)
Strite, Kenneth E. * (Washington/Baltimore)
Sweigart, Samuel (Martindale/Weaverland)
Villanueva, John (New York City)
Weaver, Alvin M. * (Lebanon and Berks Counties)
Weaver, David (Northern Pennsylvania)
Weaver, John A. * (Bedford - Oakland, Maryland)
Weaver, John M. * (Weaverland)
Weaver, John W. * (Juniata)
Weaver, Lester (Lancaster City)
Weaver, Levi H. * (Southern New York)
Weaver, Luke W. * (Martindale)
Weaver, Martin H. * (Weaverland)
Weaver, Melvin H. (Martindale)
Weaver, Melvin M. (Manheim)
Weaver, Paul N. (Groffdale)
Weaver, Rufus (Bowmansville/Reading)
Weber, Dalton L. * (Bradford)
Weber, Elmer H. * (New Danville)
Weber, Henry (Bowmansville/Reading)
Weber, Howard (Bowmansville/Reading)
Weiler, J. Mervin * (Martindale)
Wenger, Harold H. * (Chambersburg)
Wilson, Laverne (Southern New York)
Wise, Alvin G. * (Bowmansville/Reading)
Witmer, Marvin K. * (Hess-Landis Valley)
Yocum, Frederick L. * (Philadelphia City)
Yoder, John (Millwood)
Yoder, Mark * (Weaverland)
Yoder, Perry (Juniata)
Yost, Wilmer E. * (Mellinger)
Zimmerman, Alvin L. * (Cumberland)
Zimmerman, Mahlon (Florida - Tampa, Sarasota, Immokalee)
Zimmerman, Robert * (Hammer Creek)
Zimmerman, Stephen (Hammer Creek)
Zook, Howard (Washington/Baltimore)

Note: We have tried to list all present and former representatives of the Brotherly Aid Fire and Storm Plan. However, we acknowledge that someone may have been missed, because our records are incomplete. We will be glad to hear from anyone who might have been missed.

Brotherly Aid Liability Plan

General Committee/Administrative Committee

Chairman

Edwin H. Gehman	1955-1962
Harvey M. Zimmerman	1962-1966
Andrew H. Shaub	1966-1971
Paul Z. Musser	1971-1993
Andrew G. Miller	1993-present

Secretary

J. Kendig Miller	1955-1959
John B. Shenk	1960-1989
David H. Boyd	1989-1993

Secretary/Treasurer

David H. Boyd	1993-present

Treasurer

Ivan D. Leaman	1955-1993

Assistant Treasurer

A. David Buckwalter	1958-1964

Additional Member

Clayton R. Nissley	1991-1992
J. Glen Hostetler	1993-1995
Nancy L. Stauffer	1995-present

Brotherly Aid Liability Plan
Representatives

Persons who have served in the past or are continuing to serve as representatives of the Brotherly Aid Liability Plan with approximate dates when they began serving. Representatives who are active as of November 1995 are marked with an asterisk.

Acevedo, Herminio	-	July 1980
Alderfer, H. Willard & Gladys L. *	-	September 1983
Augustus, Rozlyn	-	April 1989
Baer, Gladys & Russel *	-	July 1982
Baumgarten, Dorothy	-	July 1986
Baynard, Timothy G. & Karen	-	February 1987
Bedford, Bruce	-	March 1983
Beiler, Calvin D.	-	May 1969
Beiler, Linda G. *	-	May 1988
Beiler, Melvin R. *	-	July 1982
Beiler, Vernon & Elizabeth *	-	May 1974
Belousov, Svetlana *	-	September 1995
Bergey, Curtis L.	-	May 1957
Blank, Leroy F.	-	May 1984
Boll, Mervin E.	-	May 1975
Bomberger, Clair	-	July 1971
Borisov, Paul	-	July 1991
Breneman, Daniel K.	-	June 1976
Brubaker, Dora *	-	September 1985
Brubaker, Simon A.	-	February 1963
Brunk, O.D.	-	February 1955
Buckwalter, A. David & Marian *	-	July 1963
Buckwalter, Joan E. *	-	June 1989
Burkholder, Harold E.	-	June 1959
Busz, James S.	-	April 1981
Cassel, D. Wayne *	-	January 1985
Chau, Howard K. *	-	June 1990
Clemmer, Cyrus	-	May 1957
Cross, Samuel L.	-	April 1989

DeLeon, Olga M.	-	January 1995
Detweiler, Anna Louise *	-	July 1991
Detweiler, LeRoy	-	May 1973
Diem, Ivan C.	-	December 1981
Eberly, Betty Lou *	-	August 1993
Ebersole, Ralph H. *	-	July 1986
Eby, Nancy J. *	-	January 1995
Engle, Wilbur H.	-	February 1971
Fehr, Peter *	-	June 1987
Feliciano, Rogelio	-	July 1989
Fetrow, Timothy E. *	-	September 1988
Fisher, John	-	January 1956
Forry, Wilmer R. *	-	November 1985
Frey, Gary L. *	-	April 1982
Fronheiser, Alan E.	-	July 1991
Gabriel, Leo	-	November 1985
Gagas, Sue M.	-	November 1986
Garber, Jay C.	-	July 1963
Garber, Lois A. *	-	November 1981
Garman, Lawrence W. *	-	September 1988
Gehman, Edwin	-	January 1955
Gentry, David A. & Marcia L. *	-	March 1995
Gerlach, Richard R.	-	July 1963
Ginder, Isaac S.	-	December 1963
Godshall, Paul A.	-	May 1957
Good, Lewis C., Jr.	-	February 1955
Goshow, Lucy *	-	August 1981
Graybill, Eli S.	-	November 1963
Graybill, J. Roy	-	January 1956
Groff, Daniel B.	-	October 1978
Groff, J. Lester	-	September 1990
Groff, Jacob R. *	-	January 1963
Harnish, John H.	-	January 1955
Hartzler, C. Clayton	-	May 1956
Hartzler, Steve *	-	January 1985
Hege, Paul H.	-	May 1976
Heimbach, Clair *	-	March 1979
Heimbach, Robert W. & Vicky J. *	-	July 1988
Hershberger, Terry *	-	June 1990
Hertzler, Leroy *	-	August 1955
Hertzler, Mervin W. & Ruth *	-	May 22, 1995
Hess, H. Laverne	-	May 1980
High, Ivan & Arlene	-	September 1988

Hill, Barbara E.	-	November 1986
Horning, Irvin W. & Grace *	-	May 1988
Horst, Judy L. *	-	January 1992
Horst, Leroy D.	-	August 1958
Hurst, J. Michael & Kathy *	-	January 1994
Hyland, Dorothy A. *	-	January 1993
Kane, Kennanne	-	May 1985
Kao, Paul	-	July 1991
Kauffman, C. Roscoe	-	January 1956
Kauffman, Donald S. *	-	April 1991
Kauffman, Kenneth L.	-	April 1970
Kauffman, Timothy R.	-	May 1984
Keefer, Earl E., Sr. *	-	March 1988
Kehl, Albert K. & Connie E. *	-	June 1994
Kennel, Betsy *	-	October 1994
Khuu, Peter *	-	June 1990
Kimmet, Jacqueline *	-	December 1994
King, David E.	-	May 1963
King, Eli F.	-	August 1973
King, Emerson	-	October 1987
King, Frank R.	-	May 1963
King, Harry L.	-	May 1984
King, Trennis S.	-	March 1963
Kravets, Sergey I. *	-	February 1995
Kraybill, Wilmer & Helen	-	December 1976
Kuhns, Ray E.	-	July 1973
Kurtz, Cindy L. & Richard K. *	-	September 1988
Landis, Mark G. *	-	January 1993
Lapp, David F.	-	January 1955
Lapp, Mervin E. & Ina Ruth *	-	November 1990
Lay, Vanna B. *	-	July 1993
Leaman, Ivan D.	-	January 1955
Lehman, Andrew	-	August 1958
Lehman, John & Elizabeth *	-	October 1990
Lehman, Laura F. *	-	February 1993
Leonard, Leslie	-	May 1956
Lopez, Samuel M. & Soledad *	-	May 1985
Lunchenko, Vladimir A. *	-	April 1995
Lusch, Robert	-	November 1990
Martin, Charles	-	May 1976
Martin, Crystal A.	-	July 1993
Martin, David Henry & Janet *	-	September 1981
Martin, Emanuel	-	January 1955

Martin, Ernest W. *	-	November 1990
Martin, Floyd & Janice *	-	September 1988
Martin, Hershey	-	August 1955
Martin, J. Daniel	-	September 1988
Martin, J. Paul	-	June 1989
Martin, Louise M. *	-	May 1988
Martin, Ray & Wilma *	-	May 1988
Martin, Richard Lee & Ann *	-	June 1989
Mashas, Vivian	-	May 1982
Matos, Victoriano C.	-	February 1992
Miller, Alvin B.	-	May 1985
Miller, J. Kendig	-	January 1955
Miller, J. Robert *	-	January 1984
Miron, David	-	January 1977
Molter, Nora L.	-	February 1993
Montanez, Carlos A.	-	April 1991
Montanez, Carmen M.	-	June 1993
Moyer, Elwyn L.	-	June 1979
Murphy, James T.	-	January 1981
Musser, Paul Z.	-	July 1969
Nauman, Dale E. & Martha N. *	-	January 1993
Newswanger, Debra M. *	-	August 1992
Nguyen, Ca Van	-	June 1988
Nissley, Earl E.	-	January 1955
Nyce, Wynne J.	-	January 1971
Orta, Shirley A. *	-	August 1984
Patrushev, Viktor I. *	-	October 1984
Peachey, John E.	-	May 1956
Peachey, Timothy R. & Helen L. *	-	September 1992
Perez, Milagros	-	November 1990
Petersheim, Esther L. & Arnold L. *	-	February 1995
Porter, Howard L. *	-	April 1991
Prior, Catherine E.	-	August 1981
Przywara, Joan *	-	March 1991
Putt, Barbara J.	-	November 1992
Ramos, Rafael	-	October 1977
Ranck, R. Glenn	-	September 1967
Reigner, Jonathan P. & Heidi A. *	-	April 1994
Rivera, Eduardo & Beverly *	-	November 1994
Rivera, Ruth N. *	-	April 1995
Roberts, Kenneth D. *	-	September 1988
Rohrer, John C.	-	August 1955
Ruth, Dennis H. *	-	November 1985

Sanchez, Carlos	-	October 1987
Santiago, Bartolo	-	July 1993
Sauder, Earl W. *	-	May 1988
Sauder, Martin *	-	May 1984
Schrock, Homer E.	-	February 1963
Serrano, Mario	-	January 1984
Shank, Leonard	-	August 1958
Sharp, Christ D.	-	January 1956
Siegrist, J. Sanford & Grace *	-	February 1978
Sinyagin, Leonid S.	-	September 1990
Smith, Elbert N. *	-	October 1987
Smith, Harley K.	-	November 1975
Smith, Peter	-	August 1955
Smoker, Levi S.	-	January 1955
Smoker, Omar	-	January 1980
Smoker, Wilmer S. & Ruth L. *	-	July 1978
Smucker, Amos S.	-	April 1975
Smucker, J. S.	-	June 1969
Sollenberger, Ira *	-	August 1977
Spicher, John W.	-	May 1963
Stoner, Donald E. & Clara K. *	-	June 1994
Swartz, Carl M.	-	September 1987
Sweigart, Samuel S.	-	January 1964
Taboada, Dolly	-	September 1990
Testa, Rudy G. & Donna R. *	-	January 1993
Tolentino, Arcadio	-	September 1985
Tran, Quang Xuan *	-	May 1991
Tyson, Aaron S.	-	July 1963
Vargas, Maria	-	August 1986
Vasquez, Carmen *	-	October 1995
Weaver, Alvin M. *	-	May 1958
Weaver, John W.	-	December 1970
Weaver, Joseph H.	-	January 1970
Weber, Dalton L. *	-	November 1995
Weber, Grace E.	-	May 1988
Wengerd, John *	-	June 1990
Westover, Miles D. & Connie D. *	-	February 1994
Whigham, Ertell M.	-	December 1990
Witmer, Evelyn *	-	August 1990
Yann, Monique S.	-	March 1994
Yocum, Fred L.	-	October 1976
Yoder, Amos	-	January 1955
Yoder, Earl	-	May 1956

Yoder, Kenneth J. *	-	June 1990
Yoder, Merle E. & Sallie *	-	May 1956
Yoder, Perry M.	-	January 1956
Zeager, Paul L. & Esther M. *	-	July 1978
Zendt, J. Allen & Ruth *	-	November 1981
Zendt, John H.	-	January 1956
Zimmerman, Harvey M.	-	January 1963
Zimmerman, Noah L.	-	January 1956
Zook, Lester J.	-	May 1956
Zook, Moses J.	-	July 1988

Note: We have tried to list all present and former representatives of the Brotherly Aid Liability Plan. However, we acknowledge that someone may have been missed, because our records are incomplete. We will be glad to hear from anyone who might have been missed.

Annual Meetings

The following are the dates and locations of Sharing Programs (Brotherly Aid) annual meetings.

1950	Elizabethtown Mennonite Church
1951	New Danville Mennonite Church
1952	Gingrich Mennonite Church
1953	Ephrata Mennonite Church
1954	Paradise Mennonite Church
1955	Erb Mennonite Church (First BALP Annual Meeting)
1956	Stony Brook Mennonite Church
1957	Rohrerstown Mennonite Church
1958	Stauffer Mennonite Church
1959	New Holland Mennonite Church
1960	Bossler Mennonite Church
1961	Millwood Mennonite Church
1962	Landisville Mennonite Church
1963	Gantz Mennonite Church (Grace Community Fellowship)
1964	Martindale Mennonite Church
1965	Mount Joy Mennonite Church
1966	New Providence Mennonite Church
1967	Kinzer Mennonite Church
1968	East Chestnut Street Mennonite Church
1969	Bowmansville Mennonite Church
1970	East Petersburg Mennonite Church
1971	Elizabethtown Mennonite Church
1972	Mountville Mennonite Church
1973	Willow Street Mennonite Church
1974	Krall Mennonite Church
1975	Indiantown Mennonite Church
1976	Martindale Mennonite Church
1977	Buffalo Mennonite Church
1978	New Danville Mennonite Church
1979	Chambersburg Mennonite Church

1980   Goodville Mennonite Church
1981   Mellinger Mennonite Church
1982   Lancaster Mennonite High School
1983   Mount Joy Mennonite Church
1984   Weaverland Mennonite Church
1985   Erb Mennonite Church
1986   Lancaster Mennonite High School
1987   Weaverland Mennonite Church
1988   New Holland Mennonite Church
1989 to present (1995) Lancaster Mennonite High School

Moderators or Speakers Who Served
Two or More Times at
Annual Meetings
1950 to 1979

Edwin Gehman	6
James H. Hess	6
Simon Bucher	5
Andrew Shaub	3
J. Paul Graybill	2
Clarence Lutz	2
Clarence Harnish	2
Harlan Hoover	2
Stoner Krady	2
Charles Good	2
Peter Smith	2
Homer Bomberger	2
Clayton Keener	2
Clair Eby	2
Raymond Charles	2
Willis Kling	2

Association of
Mennonite Aid Societies

The Association of Mennonite Aid Societies (AMAS) came into being in 1954, the same year Mennonite Auto Aid was founded and the same year the Brotherly Aid Liability Plan's constitution was being written. AMAS is a representative organization for counsel, promotion, education and fellowship for Mennonite, Brethren in Christ and Church of the Brethren mutual aid societies in North America.

When AMAS was formed, Fire and Storm was in operation but there is no record that it was invited to participate, although it would surely have been welcome. When AMAS began, BALP was not in operation so membership was not a question.

At the same board meeting when the board invited John Shenk to succeed in the secretarial work that Kendig Miller was doing, the board also responded positively to an invitation by Howard Raid of AMAS to visit the BALP work. Minutes of that 1959 meeting state that the board "agreed to accept the visit" of Howard Raid. However, in the spirit of keeping distance from inter-Mennonite organizations at that time, the minutes noted that "we have no interest in becoming part of the Association."

After some time of cooperation, Brotherly Aid became a full participant in AMAS. In 1992, Glen Roth was elected to serve on the AMAS Board. He was the first person from Sharing Programs to serve in this capacity.

Mennonite Indemnity, Inc.

Mennonite mutual aid companies in the 1950s discovered that they had in common a need for greater "per-risk" coverage. In 1957 a stock company called Mennonite Indemnity, Inc., was formed under the guidance of Orie Miller.

Endnotes

Introduction.

1. John and Jean Sensenig reported that 75 diverse people came to help clean up. Found in the rubble was a library book cover with only the edges burned. The title was clearly visible: *Shadrach, Meshach, and Abednego.*

Chapter 1. Before Brotherly Aid.

2. "Mutual Aid," *Mennonite Encyclopedia*, Volume III, Mennonite Publishing House, 1957.
3. "Mennonite Mutual...," *Mennonite Encyclopedia, Ibid.*
4. Paul Erb biography of Orie Miller. (Erb incorrectly attributes the founding of Brotherly Aid to Miller.)
5. Krady paper.
6. Bishop Board minutes in the Lancaster Mennonite Historical Society. Subsequent references to Bishop Board from same source.

Chapter 2. New Danville District Issues Call for Aid Plan.

7. *New Danville: Church—Community—Heritage, 1717-1992*, by Lindsay Druck Harnish (1992, published locally).
8. *Ibid.*
9. Conversation with David N. Thomas.
10. *Missionary Messenger*, the official publication of Eastern Mennonite Missions, August 1948.
11. Brotherly Aid founding minutes by James H. Hess.

Chapter 3. Special Meeting Called for February 1948

12. *Intelligencer Journal* of related dates.
13. *Light Across the Years*, Martin Ressler, editor, 1974, self-published history of the Byerland Mennonite Church, Willow Street, Pennsylvania.

14. *Mennonite Yearbook*, 1938.
15. John L. Stauffer, Eastern Mennonite University archives.
16. *History of Eastern Mennonite University* by Hubert Pellman.
17. *Weaver Bookstore*, Virginia Weaver, 1994.
18. James Hess minutes.
19. Conversation with Elmer Martin's daughter, Eunice (Mrs. Lloyd) Keller.
20. Elmer Martin in *Mellinger Mennonite Church* history.
21. Conversation with Glen A. Roth.
22. *Passing on the Faith* by Donald Kraybill, 1992.
23. First name not given in minutes.

Chapter 4. Plan Takes Shape at Vine Street.

24. James Hess minutes.
25. Conversation with David Z. Weaver.
26. James Hess minutes.
27. Correspondence with Krady's daughter, Ruth Lehman, Harrisonburg, Virginia.
28. "Mutual Aid Fire," *Mennonite Encyclopedia*, Volume III, does not refer to the origins before the chartering.

Chapter 5. Bishop Board Endorses Plan.

29. *Intelligencer Journal*, morning newspaper of the Lancaster, Pennsylvania, area, July 28, 1949.
30. In the article, "Automobile Insurance," which appeared in the October 1950 *Pastoral Messenger*, Jacob S. Buckwalter wrote: "Why should Christian people have automobile insurance? Is it a help to strengthen one's faith in God's care for His people? Is it Christlike?... I believe if we are faithful to the Lord, He will take care of us in all emergencies, or take care of the other fellow for us....I have had two collisions (both in Philadelphia), which I feel were the result of the other fellow getting me into a jam. I pulled hard away to avoid a direct hit and we edged each other over until the cars came to a stop, with injury to the machine only. In all, I paid out about $100.00 for damage which I did not think was fair." The official church magazine in the year Brotherly Aid began was running articles opposed to insurance. In only five years, articles would appear which argued that it was unfaithful to have liability because a

person wronged by a Christian may not receive full reimbursement.

Chapter 6. Fire and Storm Plan Gets Established.

31. 1950 was also the year that Christian Worker Groups (instead of Mennonite Youth Fellowships) had a Conferencewide rally. The July 1950 *Pastoral Messenger* reported how the groups were fairing in home visitation, street meetings, missionary projects, roadside evangelism, and literature distribution.
32. James Hess minutes.
33. With all the representatives present, it would seem that promotion would take care of itself. Yet in "Our Churches' Provision for the Welfare of Her Members," by J. Paul Graybill in the April 1953 *Pastoral Messenger*, Brotherly Aid was not mentioned in a long list of other programs associated with the Conference.

Chapter 7. Liability Plan Begins.

34. Behavior with cars was discussed. Girl students of the 1947-1948 Lancaster Mennonite School class wrote "Conduct I Expect of a Christian Young Man," in the January 1950 *Pastoral Messenger*: "I do not think a Christian young man will race around on Sunday, burning up gas without a purpose. A Christian man is also respected when he refrains from buying ice cream and other things on Sunday.... When a young man wants a date, he should go to the door of her home and there meet her instead of making her come out to his car to see him."
35. Data taken from a common *Almanac* of the year mentioned.
36. *Passing on the Faith, Ibid,* page 94.
37. James Hess minutes.
38. Amos Horst wrote such brief minutes of Bishop Board minutes that it is possible to read a discrepancy between his minute and what Krady reported to the Brotherly Aid Board. Krady, Elmer Martin, and Simon Bucher could not have likely reported an action that did not take place.

Chapter 8. The Cottage Years

39. As recently as the October 1951 *Pastoral Messenger*, an article by "a Mennonite Doctor," stated that, "As a physician I could not conscientiously take out malpractice insurance to prevent my patients from suing me. For the same reason, I cannot see that our brotherhood is consistent for agreeing more or less in taking automobile insurance since this is not required by law as is commonly believed." Of course, taking out insurance does not prevent lawsuits; that rationale is also flawed linking the two different kinds of insurance.

40. Data taken from a common *Almanac* of the year mentioned.

41. Conversations with J. Kendig Miller, 1994.

42. Minutes of the Brotherly Aid Liability Plan of the date mentioned.

43. *Intelligencer Journal*, morning newspaper of the Lancaster, Pennsylvania area, of the date mentioned.

44. Conversation with James Lapp, 1994.

45. Conversation with Elton Moshier, 1994.

46. Personal letter in James Hess file.

Chapter 9. Some Founders Retire.

47. Conversation with J. Kendig Miller.

48. On February 10, 1962, the Gantz Meetinghouse suffered $12,000 in fire damage (see April 1962 *Mennonite Research Journal*).

Chapter 10. John B. Shenk Joins Liability Team.

49. Conversation with Paul G. Landis, 1994.

50. Conversation with John B. Shenk, 1994.

51. Personal records of Elton Moshier.

Chapter 11. Hospital Bills and Burdens to Share.

52. *Almanac.*

Chapter 12. Mennonite Brotherly Aid Office Opens.

53. Of course, the plans had already been approved by the Bishop Board, but after 15 years, their administration by the Conference had lapsed into assumptions.
54. This in sharp contrast to Orie Miller's letter to Amos Horst of May 3, 1950, stating regret and apology "for the unintended sending of Mennonite Aid, Inc., publicity material into the Lancaster Conference District." The same letter of apology was sent to Truman Brunk of Virginia Conference and Jacob Clemens of Franconia Conference.

Chapter 13. Mennonite Brotherly Aid Office Prospers.

55. John Shenk written report to BALP after trip.
56. Conversation with John Shenk, 1994.
57. Quotes from Vernon Charles' written memoirs.

Chapter 14. No-fault Law Forces a Choice.

58. Mennonite Mutual Aid Collection, Archives of the Mennonite Church, Goshen, Indiana.
59. Letter from Edgar Stoesz to John Shenk, June 22, 1973.

Index

— A —

Accrual accounting, 123
Air Force, 69
Alabama, 36
Allegheny Conference, 80
Alternative Service: I-W, 69
Amish, 38
Amish Aid and Fire Insurance Company, 21
Amish Fire Company, 1
Anabaptist, x, 1, 11
Andes, Paul, 13
Archives Library, 81
Association of Mennonite Aid Societies, 63, 98, 171
Atlantic Coast Conference, 119

— B —

Bally-Boyertown, 36
Barn raisings, 1
Beachy Amish, 80
Beidler, Stanley, 34, 36
Beiler, Isaac and Naomi, 79
Belleville, Pennsylvania, 26, 69, 80
Bender, Harold S., x
Bergey, Bonnie, 116
Bishop Board, 4, 5, 6, 7, 10, 11, 15, 21, 22, 23, 27,
    51, 55, 60, 72, 84, 85, 91, 92, 93, 94
Blossom Hill Mennonite Church, 113
Bluffton, Ohio, 81
Board of Brotherhood Ministries, 115
Bomberger, Homer, 38
Book, Parke, 31, 34
Boshart, Lloyd, 85, 106
Bowmansville Mennonite Church, 103
Boyd, David, 114, 115, 116, 118, 124

— C —

— D —

— **H** —

— I —

— J —

— K —

Old Order Mennonite, 80, 119
Oreville Mennonite Home, 6, 20, 43, 54

— P —

Paradise District, 53, 113
Pastoral Messenger, 27, 43
Peifer, Monroe, 88
Pellman, Hubert, 14
Pennsylvania Safety Responsibility Act, 52
Petersheim, Judy, 118
Philhaven, 38, 63, 84
Pierce, Lois, 116, 118
Plains Mennonite Church, 18
Provident Bookstore, 80

— R —

Raid, Howard, 81, 82
Ramos, Rafael, 113, 114
Rawlinsville Mennonite Church, 6, 11, 97
Reber, Joseph, 44
Reber, Rebecca, 44
Ressler, Dale, 116, 118, 121, 124
Ressler, Martin, 57
Revolutionary War, 14
Rheam, James, 88
Rhodes, Gretchen, 118
Risser, John D., 21
Risser, Noah, 5, 34, 46
River Corner Mennonite Church, 11
Roberts, Kenneth D., 128
Rohrer, Clarence, 72
Rohrer, Earl W., 66, 76
Rohrerstown Mennonite Church, 3, 24, 45
Rossmere Mennonite Church, 77
Roth, Glen A., 15, 118, 121, 124, 130
Rush, Sue, 118, 120

— S —

Safety Responsibility Act, 42